HELP!

I'm Raising My Grandkids

Grandparents Adapting to Life's Surprises

HELP! I'M RAISING MY GRANDKIDS: GRANDPARENTS ADAPTING TO LIFE'S SURPRISES

By Harriet Hodgson, BS, MA

ISBN-10: 1475068409
ISBN-13: 9781475068405

Cover design by Jay Highum,
Action Graphic Design, Rochester, Minnesota, USA.

Photo source: www.istockphoto.com

The information in this book is not intended to serve as a replacement for professional advice or counseling. Any use of the information in this book is at the reader's discretion. The author and publisher specifically disclaim any and all liability arising directly or indirectly from the use or application of any information contained in this book. A medical professional should be consulted regarding a specific situation.

To learn more about this busy author and grandmother, please visit

www.harriethodgson.com

HELP!

I'm Raising My Grandkids

Grandparents Adapting to Life's Surprises

Harriet Hodgson, BS, MA
Foreword by Kenneth J. Doka, PhD

Dedication

This book is dedicated to my daughter,
Helen Anne Hodgson Welby, mother of my twin grandchildren.
You are in my heart and always will be.

Contents

of Kindness * Expectations: Yours and Theirs * Online Communities
and Blogs * Evaluating Internet Articles

Chapter 8: Fostering Children's Goals and Dreams, 119

Good Food is Brain Food * Sleepovers and Getting Your Zs *
Learning to Laugh Again * Your Happiness Link * Importance
of Play * Creative Outlets * Goal Setting is a Sign of Progress *
Reaching Goals Takes Team Effort * Balloons: Charting Progress *
Letting Go Again * Are You Still You? * It's All about Love

Maximizing This Book

Reading is a luxury for many grandparents who are raising their grandchildren. Hundreds of books, pamphlets and articles are available, yet you have little or no time to read them. Though you set aside time for reading, the best-laid plans often go astray, and you may read this book in snatches.

You may also read when you're too tired to recall information. That's why this book is written and designed for easy reading. It's manageable, not too thick, not too thin, and written in a conversational style. The headings are like guideposts that lead you through the chapters. Here are some tips to help you get the most from this book.

1. Scan the headings before you read the chapter.
2. Make the book yours and write notes in white spaces and margins.
3. Check the "Words to Know" section.
4. Share your caregiving ideas and concerns with trusted people.
5. Join a support group.
6. Discuss chapter topics and sub-topics at support group meetings.
7. Take advantage of online support communities and blogs.

8. Stay in touch with other grandparents who are raising grandkids.
9. Accept your feelings of loss and grief.
10. Try some of the caregiving tips.
11. Loan the book to other grandparents or give them a copy.
12. Remember, raising grandkids is all about love.

Foreword

Let me begin with open disclosure. I am a grandparent. I have two grandchildren. Kenny, age eight years at this writing, and Lucy, now five years old. I was deeply honored when my son, Michael, and his wife, Angelina, named their first child after me. Both children are a joy to me. I live close to them and do all the grandparent things – taking them to school on days that I am home, babysitting on a moment's notice, helping with homework, buying gifts, and watching their games and competitions.

Research has supported the important role of the grandparent. Grandparents can be a critical resource to the child and parent, offering time, talent, and treasure to their grandchild. They can receive much as well — a sense of biological and familial continuity, the stimulation of being with a young child, seeing the world anew through that child's eyes, and the sense of vicarious achievement in the small and large accomplishments of the grandchild.

Like many grandparents, I enjoy the role. And like many grandparents, I especially enjoy the limited and privileged involvement often identified with the role. A brief anecdote may describe it. When Kenny was three years old, he was in the backseat of my car as we picked up pizza for a family supper. I noticed Kenny nervously looking out the back window. In response to my question, Kenny warned, "You have to be careful, Grandpa. The moon can follow you home." I was fascinated with the response and Kenny then taught me all about space. The stars, it seems, are very far up and you need one, maybe two, big ladders to reach them. You have to be careful though; they are hot like light bulbs. After Kenny went to sleep, I recounted the story to my son and daughter-in-law. My son laughed and reminded me that he would have received a lecture on astronomy. He was right. We often teach our children, but learn from our grandchildren. It is a very difficult relationship. Like the old saw says, we spoil them and give them back to their parents. And quite frankly, as much as I enjoy them, I also enjoy after a day, giving them back. In my 60s, they can exhaust me.

What happens, though, when you cannot give them back? What happens when situations such as divorce, death, or economic upheaval, create a situation where grandparents have to raise their grandchildren? Almost one out of ten grandparents has this role, either raising or having a significant role in raising a grandchild. Such a situation is wrought with complications.

First, grandparents raising grandchildren inevitably results from some form of loss – a child dies, divorces, loses a job, falls to addiction, or has physical or mental health difficulties. So grandparents must not only deal with their own disappointments and grief, but also the grief of their grandchildren. They are truly wounded healers.

Second, the reality is that as one ages, it is difficult to cope with the boundless energy of a child, the inherent drama of an adolescent, and the unceasing demands of parenthood. It is exhausting. Moreover, at a time when sources of income may be more limited, the expenses of raising a child can be daunting.

Third, one's sense of an assumptive world is challenged. This is not the way it is supposed to be. Both grandparent and grandchild have to deal with the constant incongruity inherent to this context. That too, is a source of grief. This grief is often disenfranchised, that is, un-acknowledged by others, perhaps even one's self. It is difficult, outside of a support group, to really explore the inherent ambivalence of such a role. It is equally difficult to be pitied for raising grandchildren, or unrealistically portrayed as a saint, when all you are doing is coping with the hand you were dealt.

Happily, Harriet Hodgson's book, ***Help! I'm Raising My Grandkids***, will be a most useful resource to grandparents in that role and those who seek to understand and assist them. Hodgson offers not only critical validation, but practical suggestions to navigate this difficult terrain. Hodgson writes from her experience. In her 70s, the sudden deaths of her daughter and former son-in-law brought her 15-year-old grandchildren to her door. In some ways, her situation may be construed as atypical. Hodgson had resources to draw upon, as both she and her husband were educated professionals, happily married, and reasonably prosperous. The twins, though dealing with sudden loss, seemed stable and well-adjusted. Yet they were still thrown into the tumult of a life suddenly changed. In recounting her struggles, Hodgson offers counsel that transcends any differences of class, ethnicity, or circumstances. Not only are Hodgson's story and advice useful, she has also packed the book with additional resources, such as organizations and Internet support for grandparents now thrust into a parenting role.

Raising grandchildren is challenging even in the best of situations and circumstances. Yet Hodgson's book makes it a little less lonely, offering critical reassurance, even when one does not have the freedom to give children back to their parents.

—Kenneth J. Doka, PhD, Professor, The Graduate School,
The College of New Rochelle, and Senior Consultant,
The Hospice Foundation of America

Introduction

When the phone rang I was just drifting off to sleep. The jarring sound awakened me instantly. Who would be calling at this hour? "Hello," I answered tentatively.

"There's been an accident," the caller said. "Your granddaughter was injured and taken to the hospital by ambulance. Your daughter was injured and taken to the hospital by helicopter. Her injuries are really bad."

I shared this news with my husband. We dressed quickly and drove to the hospital emergency department. Our granddaughter had a mild concussion and our daughter was in surgery. As the hours passed, more surgeons were called in to assist. Twenty hours later we received the news we had been dreading; our daughter was brain dead.

We signed legal documents to cease medical support and donate our daughter's organs. Then we went into surgery to say good-bye. Our granddaughter, who had been dismissed from the emergency room, came with us, along with our grandson. They're fraternal twins and our only grandchildren. Blunt force trauma had caused my daughter's face to swell and she didn't look like herself. The twins stood beside the gurney and sobbed uncontrollably. I wondered if they would survive such tragedy. Would I?

Our former son-in-law offered to move into the house with the twins and live with them until they graduated from high school. Since we were older adults, we accepted his offer.

Life had changed and everyone in the family tried to change with it. A week after their mother died the twins, with support from their father, decided to return to high school. Months passed, and though we tried to live normal lives, a pall of sadness followed each of us. Katie Dog (Dog was her last name), the family's beloved Cocker Spaniel, missed my daughter so much she went into the bedroom closet and stayed there.

Nobody in the family, least of all the dog, knew there was more tragedy to come. Two days after my daughter died, my father-in-law succumbed to pneumonia. Two months later my brother had a heart attack and died. In the fall, my former son-in-lad died from the injuries he received in another car crash. My granddaughter called to tell us about the accident. We picked up the twins at their house and took them to the hospital. Other relatives were waiting in a special room for family members. A few minutes we learned my former son-in-law had died.

"Why is this happening to us?" my granddaughter sobbed. I couldn't answer her question.

As we were leaving the hospital I turned to the twins and announced, "You're coming home with us." With the clarity that comes in crisis, I knew caring for them was my new life mission, a mission my husband and I shared. Ours was a sacred mission and we didn't know where it would lead. This book is the story of that journey, my role as a grandparent raising grandchildren, the challenges I faced, the solutions I found, and the joy I have experienced.

Shortly after our grandkids moved in with us I realized we needed help and called the local Department of Social Services. To my dismay, I found the support group for grandparents had disbanded. Where could I turn? I turned to relatives, friends, books, articles, and my child development degree from Wheelock College. If you had told me I would be using this degree in my 70s I would have said you were delusional. But I've used this training again and again and Wheelock's philosophy of putting the child first has helped me immensely.

I wish I could afford a full-page thank-you ad in a major newspaper, but I can't, so I thank my alma mater here. Graduating from Wheelock College changed my life and shaped my grandchildren's lives. Thank you Wheelock!

Relatives suggested I write a book about my life as a GRG, grandparent raising grandchildren. "Do it for the family," my brother-in-law advised. Though I thought about the idea, I didn't act on it because of the challenges it presented, with confidentiality at the top of the list. Rabbi Earl Grollman changed my mind. He had written a mini-review for the cover of my previous book and liked the book so much he called several times. "You're a good writer," he said. "You should write about raising your grandchildren."

My feelings swung back and forth like a pendulum. Yes I'll write it. No I won't. Yes I'll write it. No I won't. I thought about Rabbi Grollman's suggestion for weeks and figured out how to do it. I would tell a personal story, weave research findings into the story, and add as many practical tips as possible. I am grateful to Rabbi Grollman for his encouragement and kindness.

The title of the book comes from my life, for there were times when I wanted to stand in the center of the mall and shout, "Help! I'm raising my grandkids. Got any ideas?" It wouldn't be a wimpy shout; it would be a top-of-my lungs shout. You've probably wanted to call for help as well. This book is packed with tips for all grandparents who are raising grandkids and the journey we share. During this journey you will:

- See what's behind the GRG trend
- Recognize your losses
- Define your GRG responsibilities and tasks
- Stock up on communication tips
- Learn how to go "back" to school
- Deal with the stressors that awaken you
- Build a new life with your grandchildren
- Foster your grandchildren's goals and dreams.

Ten percent of all the grandparents in the nation are raising their grandchildren and the number is going up. Two acronyms have come from this trend, GRG for grandparents raising grandchildren, and GAP for grandparents as parents. The purpose of this book is to make your life easier, and each chapter closes with a list of proven tips. Just look for the "What Works" headings.

The reading time for the book is about three hours, but the impact cannot be measured now. Only time can do that. You've joined a club, the Grandparents Raising Grandchildren Club, and it's one of the best you'll ever join. Indeed, it will change your life. Miles separate us, yet we are not alone. We are linked together, loving our grandchildren, caring for them, protecting them, enjoying them, and rooting for the next generation. What a blessing!

1

WHAT'S BEHIND THE TREND?

Grandparents raising grandchildren has been a growing trend for years. As the trend spread, state after state developed programs to help GRGs and GAPs, creating support groups, booklets, pamphlets, conferences, and blogs. Many grandparents are raising grandchildren because their own children got into trouble, something that's hard to admit. Indeed, it is a source of ongoing emotional pain.

HOW DID YOU GET HERE?

Becoming a GRG can be an instant change, like mine, or a gradual one. You may have worried about your child (the parent of your grandchild) for years, witnessing drug experimentation, drug/alcohol addiction, risky behaviors, sexual activity, sexual promiscuity, petty theft, and running with the wrong crowd. Each morning you awakened with the hope that your child would choose a better path. That day never came.

Like fog lifting in early morning, the fog cleared from your mind, and you realized you had to take action. If your child wasn't going to care for children, you would. So you revved up your parenting instincts and stepped forward, committing your life to grandchildren though the road is long, the burden is heavy, and the shock is great.

A "Chicago Tribune" article describes the shock Sandra and Terry Eck felt when their son called and asked his parents to care for his 22-month old son. "Of course we said yes," Sandra is quoted as saying. "The alternative was foster care." Agreeing to raise their grandson turned the couple's lives upside down. "We were in a total state of shock having to start all over with a little one," Sandra continued. Yet the Ecks are convinced they made the right decision.

My husband and I also made the right decision. Our daughter was a difficult child and her high school years were troubled ones. Life gave us the opportunity to replace painful memories with happier ones. When I told the twins they were coming home with us, I didn't say anything about my doubts. Could I do this at age 72? How would the kids feel about leaving their home? Would I have enough energy for the job?

But when I had a chance to think about becoming a GRG, I realized I was on the winning team. First, I had a degree in child development. Second, I had raised teenagers before. Third, I had written about teenagers and this research would be helpful. Fourth, my husband and I were devoted to each other and had a loving and calm home, something the twins really needed. Fifth, I had many life experiences to draw upon and the wisdom that comes with age.

You're on a winning team as well. Even if you're a team of one, you're on it, and making a difference in children's lives. There's no substitute for love and you have plenty to give. There's no substitute for food, clothing, and shelter and you can provide these on your own or with financial assistance.

Kids need structure to feel secure and you're providing that, too. Whether you like it or not, you've become part of a national and international trend and are in the company of millions. In fact, you are connected to people across the nation and around the world.

REASONS FOR THE TREND

Why are so many grandparents raising their grandkids? The American Academy of Child and Adolescent Psychiatry lists the reasons for this national trend in its article, "Grandparents Raising Grandchildren," and they are:

- Increasing number of single-parent families
- The high divorce rate
- Teen pregnancy
- AIDS (Acquired Immune Deficiency Syndrome)
- Incarceration of parent(s)
- Parents are on drugs
- Parental abuse and neglect
- Death or disability of parents.

You may be raising grandkids for a combination of reasons. An addicted parent may be looking for the next fix and not looking out for children. A single parent may have a terminal disease. Immature parents may suddenly realize that child-rearing is lots of work and run away.

David M. Allen, MD, writes about the influence of personality in his article, "A Matter of Personality." Published in "Psychology Today," the article says some grandparents are raising grandchildren because of external factors such as "the sudden unemployment of parents, military parents being deployed to Iraq, or the untimely death or serious illness of the child's parents. . ."

The sagging economy has also influenced this trend. But the hardest reason is the death of a child.

Children's feelings about their parents may add to your burden. As Alan Wolfelt, PhD explains in his article, "Helping Teenagers Cope With Grief," the timing of death affects children. "If a parent dies while the adolescent is emotionally and physically pushing the parent away," he writes, "there is often a sense of guilt and 'unfinished business.'"This complicates the recovery process and caregiving.

My twin grandchildren were 15 years old when their mother died and 15 ¾ years old when their father died. Every age is a terrible age to lose a parent, but this age is particularly hard. Teens are vulnerable and changeable. Their behavior can switch dramatically in just a few minutes. Knowing we would have little time for each other, my husband and I made our grandchildren a top priority. "We're drawing on the marriage bank account," I commented, and my husband agreed.

As I reflect on the five years the twins have lived with us, I realize our roles were easier because our daughter and grandchildren lived in the same town. Their parents' divorce was very hard on the twins. Our daughter wanted more contact with us and asked to come for dinner every Sunday. We agreed instantly. This helped our daughter because she didn't have to fix a meal and received the emotional support she needed. Our Sunday dinners were special and remembering them comforts me today.

When the twins first moved in with us we couldn't help but wonder what they were thinking. Did they remember happy times with their parents or conflicting times? Were their memories accurate? Even if their memories were sketchy, the twins had witnessed conflict between their mother and father. My daughter and her husband had different goals, different views on money management, and different parenting styles. Though my daughter converted to her husband's religion, it didn't work out, and she began to explore other faiths. As time passed the differences between these two kind people became so great they divorced.

FAMILY CONFLICTS AND COPING WITH THEM

Divorce is one of the main reasons grandparents are raising their grandchildren. Your new role is a challenge and so is your child's divorce. The best thing you can do for yourself (and your grandkids) is to stay out of the way and not take sides. K. R. Tremblay and colleagues write about the divorce dilemma in their article, "Grandparents: As Parents," posted on the Colorado State University Extension website. "It is in the grandchild's best interest to keep matters as amicable as possible," they note.

Expanding on this point, the authors also say grandparents should not let themselves be used as a divorce weapon. "These attempts should be resisted, and dealt with in an open manner." After our daughter divorced, my husband and I continued to be courteous to our former son-in-law. We discussed issues with our daughter and provided emotional support, but never in the presence of the twins.

Susan Adox speaks about family conflicts in her article, "Grandparents as parents: GRGs/GAPs Have Major Issues to Resolve." She says raising grandchildren changes family relationships. "If the situation is the result of one child being an irresponsible parent, other siblings may feel that their sibling is being rewarded for bad behavior." What's more, they may think the grandchildren who are living in the house are favored over grandchildren living elsewhere. Non-residential grandchildren may show their feelings by acting out.

Kids who move in with their grandparents make sacrifices. They may move to a new neighborhood, sleep in a different bed, eat different food, and adapt to new schedules. Grandchildren may not be able to spend as much time with friends as they did previously. Text messaging and phone calls help, but nothing replaces personal contact. You need to do all you can to help your grandchildren stay in touch with supportive friends.

GUILT, THE MONSTER IN THE ROOM

Monsters are the subject of many children's books and the monster is usually under the bed or hiding in a closet. Ongoing guilt is the grandparenting monster and it fills the room. Guilt is non-productive and, in the long run, a waste of time. It can lead to poor decisions, such as buying too many toys for children and not enforcing your house rules.

Rochester, Minnesota, has a curfew, and when we didn't want the twins to stay out late with friends, we cited the law. When they were older, however, around age 17, we let them go to a midnight premier of the latest Harry Potter movie. By then we trusted the twins and they trusted us. Though they would never say it, they know we have their welfare at heart.

Guilt is a problem for grandparents of all races but, according to the National Grandparents Raising Grandchildren

Examiner website, it is a special problem for African Americans. Kathy Gaillard cites the guilt issue in her article, "More African American Grandparents are Raising Grandchildren." According to Gaillard, a disproportionate number of GRGs are African American, a trend that reflects the "unspoken understanding that you 'take care of your own.'"

Gaillard goes on to say that African American grandparents who are raising their grandchildren consider the role "to be a stigma and shame for the entire family." Worse, some African American GRGs feel they are to blame for their children's problems, a feeling I suspect is shared by grandparents of many cultures. Guilt can be a form of regret, a wish to turn back the clock, and you may slip into "If only I had . . ." thinking. Before you know it, this kind of thinking is out of control.

Rabbi Earl A. Grollman brings up regret in his book, *Straight Talk About Death for Teenagers.* "Blaming yourself and others won't bring him or her back to life," he explains. Similarly, blaming yourself (guilt feelings) won't make up for your child's poor behavior, so you may as well cast it aside and move on. If you don't cast guilt aside it will hold you back.

Self-blame is a sticky place and you can get stuck there for years. Guilt takes up too much space in your mind and in your life, and you need to get rid of it. The question is, "How?" You may start by focusing on the present, asking for help, joining a support group, staying socially connected, and practicing self-care. This isn't easy, but you have to take care of yourself in order to care for grandkids.

Your grandkids may also feel guilty. Circumstances vary, and young children may feel like they are living with you because they didn't "measure up" or weren't "good enough."

Abusive parents may use these points to get what they want and stay in control. But you're the adult in charge and you can keep reassuring grandchildren that they're worthy, deserve to be safe, and deserve to be happy.

BEHAVIOR PROBLEMS

We are fortunate grandparents, for when our twin grand-children moved in with us they understood family values, hard work, and the benefits of education. They also had good manners. The first night they were with us, overcome with grief as they were, each left the table and said, "Thank you Grandma." Hearing this made me want to cry and I couldn't believe they remembered their manners during this time of crisis.

Unfortunately, some grandparents are caring for emotionally disturbed children. As the American Academy of Child and Adolescent Psychiatry explains in its article, "Grandparents Raising Grandchildren," many of the children who are living with their grandparents "arrive with preexisting problems or risk factors, including abuse, neglect, prenatal exposure to drugs and alcohol, and the loss of parents (death, abandonment and incarceration)."

The American Association for Marriage and Family Therapy makes a similar point in a website article about GRGs. "Because of their experiences with their parents, children being raised in grandparent-headed families often display developmental, physical, behavioral, academic, and emotional problems." Your grandchildren may be depressed, have anxiety issues, Attention Deficit Disorder (ADD), learning disabilities, or aggressive behavior.

Babies may show they're upset by being fussy, crying more than usual and banging their heads. Toddlers may show they're upset by regressing. Potty-trained toddlers may begin soiling themselves, sucking their thumbs, and imitating babies. It's frustrating to see a toddler who knows many words regress and start saying, "Wah, wah." Caring for grandchildren is hard enough without these complications.

Young children may be calmed with water play, washing their hands in tepid water, and having a warm or cold drink. Older children may be calmed with physical activities: basketball, stick ball, soccer, and other sports. Adolescents may be calmed with projects, diversionary activities like a picnic or weekend trip, movies and CDs.

Seeing a pediatrician also helps. He or she may refer you to organizations and colleagues who specialize in specific areas of medicine. You may turn to a child psychiatrist, a psychologist, or support groups. Before you contact a professional, keep a log of your grandchild's behavior. Note the date, the situation, and describe the behavior as concisely as you can. You may also find helpful resources at the public library.

KIDS LOVE YOU AND ARE EMBARRASSED BY YOU

Embarrassment can be a big issue for grandchildren. Though grandchildren appreciate your efforts and the love and safety of your home, your age can make them uncomfortable. Linda Dannison, PhD, CFLE and Andrea B. Smith, PhD, LSW, describe grandchildren's embarrassment in their Family Information Services website article, "Understanding Emotional Issues in Your Grandchildren's Lives." Grandchildren may feel exposed and sensitive about living with their grandparents. "Comments and questions from other children may be difficult for them to manage," the authors explain.

This is easy to understand. Grandparents look different, have different experiences, different values, different clothes, different words, different humor, different interests, and different goals. These differences make you stand out from the crowd, as this story shows.

Our granddaughter had been a member of the gymnastics team for years. Shortly after she moved into our house the team held a parents' night, a time to thank parents for their support. Fortunately, our granddaughter gave us fair warning about this custom. "Tonight is parents' night," she explained. "Someone will say your names and I'll give you a flower."

When the girls lined up for the ceremony, I was dismayed to see the team was arranged by height and my diminutive granddaughter was first. We were introduced as her grandparents and our granddaughter walked toward us. She was smiling, but I wondered if she wanted to cry. I know I did, because I missed my daughter so much. I smiled instead.

We continued to go to meets and were obviously the oldest couple there. A little girl, about two years old, often sat near us. She walked up to me and announced, "You Grandma." I agreed with her and thought the issue was closed. It wasn't. She made this announcement several times during each gymnastic meet and continued to say it until the season ended. After this experience I had no doubt, no doubt whatsoever, that I was a senior citizen.

Children who live with their grandparents also face a stigma. Kids can be cruel and say things like, "You live with those old folks?" It's hard to reply to comments like these and children may stuff their feelings. Still, you have time and love on your side. The time may come when you can discuss this stigma and embarrassment with your grandchildren. Pick an appropriate time, an appropriate place, and keep your message short.

RESPONDING TO COMMENTS

Most people don't know what to say to folks like us. I've received many kind comments and comments that make me wince. One person told me raising my grandchildren assured me a seat in heaven. Our granddaughter told us a story about her driving instructor. He wondered why we drove them to lessons, and they answered honestly. "He thinks you are saints," she told us. Oh dear.

A friend who has known us for years describes us as "wounded healers." Her description is more accurate. Multiple losses have wounded us, yet we are strong, enjoying our lives and our grandchildren. "They're wonderful," my husband keeps saying. We aren't saints and we aren't reserving seats in heaven. Like millions of other GRGs and GAPs, we're older adults who love our grandchildren and want them to be happy. People who compliment us are trying to give us credit for our efforts. Yet it's difficult to reply. I've narrowed my responses down to two, "Thank you" and "Thank you for thinking of us."

Despite years of experience, grandparents falter every once in a while. The problem with comments that make us sound like super heroes and heroines is that people may be disappointed if we stumble, blunder, or make mistakes. My husband and I are simply doing what grandparents are supposed to do. Only you can decide how to respond to comments and how much you believe them.

Raising grandchildren is often the source of family squabbles. Some relatives may give you well-meaning advice you don't want or need. Others may criticize your caregiving, something you don't need either. Minor squabbles can grow into bitter fights that divide a family for years. Once a family is divided, it's hard to put it back together. I encourage you to do all you can to avoid confrontational arguments. Get some back-up if you need it – a family mediator, professional counselor, clergy, or lawyer. You may also attend a grandparenting seminar or conference.

MAKING SACRIFICES

Grandparents who are raising their grandchildren make sacrifices. Some have to give up their jobs. Others work part-time. Still others have to find less expensive housing. In our land of plenty, many GRGs and GAPs live in poverty. Their dreams of moving to a better place or getting a reliable car are gone. For these caregivers, each day is a struggle to survive.

You may be one of these grandparents. In my experience, it's possible to make sacrifices and retain your sense of self. Friends told me I'd have to give up writing in order to care for my grandchildren. Giving up writing would seem like another death in the family, and it would be mine. I decided to keep writing, no matter what. Usually I got up at six in the morning, but to have time for writing I got up at five and wrote in my pajamas. Then I gave the twins breakfast and my husband drove them to school. After I was dressed for the day I resumed writing.

The decision to keep writing is one of the best decisions I ever made. It saved me from resentment and anger. Writing early in the morning worked so well I still write at the crack of dawn, when the house is so quiet I can almost hear it breathe, when my thoughts are fresh and racing, when my energy level is high.

My husband made a significant sacrifice. Several years ago he retired from medical practice, yet continued to work on a contract basis. Part-time employment suited him well and kept him connected to the profession he loves so much. But he was also managing six estates: his mother's estate, his father's estate, our deceased daughter's estate, the twin's estates, and our own estate. The paperwork load was so overwhelming he retired fully. Necessary as this decision was, I think it made him sad.

According to the American Association for Marriage and Family Therapy, grandparents who are raising grandchildren have less time for themselves. "They may also have less time to spend with their partners and friends. This loss of time can be stressful and cause feelings of anger, grief, and loss."

Lenora M. Poe, PhD, a marriage, family and child therapist in Berkeley, California, writes about sacrifices, describing them as losses and gains in her article, "Connecting the Bridges: Grandparenting Grandchildren." Poe thinks grandparents can become emotionally overwhelmed. Some make comparison lists, with losses on the left and gains on the right. For example, the loss of leisure time is listed as a loss. Gains are listed across from this loss and they include involvement in education, little league, and scouting.

In the passing years, I've thought about losses and gains many times and made a list of them. Your losses and gains may be similar to mine or quite different. Here's my list of comparisons.

LOSSES	GAINS
Loss of a quiet house	Hearing my granddaughter practice choir music (she has a clear, pure voice) is a joy. Best of all, I hear the sound of children's laughter.
Lack of privacy	Our house turned out to have an ideal layout for our new family. The twins close their doors when they want privacy and we close ours.
Hurried, irregular dinners due to gymnastics	I enjoyed all of these activities, especially the meets, band and choir concerts holiday concerts and the marching band concerts.
Inability to do things at the last minute	The time I've spent with my grandchildren has helped me to know them, understand them, and feel close to them.
Waiting for the washer and dryer	My grandchildren are doing their own laundry and understand Laundry 101 because they live here.

A dented, dinged car	I provided transportation when the twins needed it.
Fewer social contacts and loneliness	I'm making a difference in the twin's lives and helping them craft their futures.
Less time for my husband	This makes the time we have together even more precious and we still go out on dates.
Energy drain and fatigue	Grandchildren appreciate my efforts. Thankfully, after 12 years in the classroom I know how to pace myself.

Create your own comparison list. Does it contain any surprises? Keep the list and add to it later, if necessary.

Interestingly, when I typed the header for this manuscript, I made a mistake. Instead of listing my last name and the title of the book, I typed my last name and *Help! I'm Saving My Grandkids*. Some people would say this is a Freudian slip. Others would say it's the truth. Time and again, family members have expressed amazement at the twin's progress and credited us for it. "We have to give the twins credit too," is my reply.

According to Poe, children need to know they have a home to return to, "someone there to receive them, a bed to sleep in, a table to sit and eat, and someone to hug and say, 'I love you. You are special.'" We have provided these things for our grandchildren. In the future, if something happens to one of us, the other will continue to provide a home.

ETHNIC GROUPS AND BARRIERS

The American Association of Retired Persons (AARP) studied the GRG trend and presented its findings in a report titled "Lean On Me: Support and Minority Outreach for Grandparents Raising Grandchildren." The report deals with Hispanic, African American, and Native American groups. According to the report, the "fastest growing segment of children living in grandparent-headed homes are Hispanic, with the African American segment close behind."

Many grandparents in these ethnic groups have little or no information about the support services available to them. So it's not surprising that these grandparents feel stressed and alone. While African American grandparents may tap informal support networks, Hispanics and Native Americans are less apt to do so because of the barriers they face. These barriers include lack of transportation, lack of child care, lack of information, and the isolation of Native American reservations. Some grandparents are influenced by a culture which says, "We take care of our own."

Government census figures show the percentage of Asian grandparents raising their grandchildren is low, only three percent. Grandparenting customs vary from one Asian culture to another and this number may not reflect the reality of their lives. In some cultures, the grandmother is responsible for child care during the first months of a baby's life. As Susan Adcox explains in her article, "Asian Grandparents

Have Influence, Status," Asian families are generally more hierarchical than American families. "Grandparents often take on the responsibility of teaching their grandchildren the language and traditions of the homelands."

Clearly, more research is needed on ethnic grandparents who are raising their grandchildren.

If you haven't looked into community support, now may be the time to do it. Contact your religious community, the local hospital or clinic, or Department of Social Services for more information. Visit the AARP website and read "Lean on Me" by Curt Davies and Dameka Williams. Talk with other GRGs and GAPs in your community.

WHAT WORKS

- Refrain from taking sides in a divorce.
- Discuss thorny issues in private.
- Make sacrifices willingly.
- Help grandchildren stay in touch with their friends
- Remember, you're the adult.
- Become aware of grandparenting barriers.

2

SHADOWS OF GRIEF IN YOUR LIFE

When you're in crisis it's easy to slip into victim thinking. You may spend hours wondering why this happened to you and why it happened now. As someone who has been through many crises, I can tell you this thinking is a waste of time. Later, after life has settled down a bit, you may wish to think about these things, but right now you need to be realistic and strong.

Every grandparent who is raising their grandchildren is grieving. You may be grieving for deceased child, a wayward child, or the vulnerable children in your care. Maybe you're experiencing anticipatory grief, a feeling of loss before a death or dreaded event occurs. Something terrible is going to happen, you just know it, but you don't know what and you don't know when. Helpless as you feel, you keep putting one foot in front of the other and doing what grandparents do.

Grief has been compared to a roller coaster ride and it's a good comparison. I've been on that ride and it was too long. Thankfully, I was able to get off the roller coaster, do my grief work, and create a new and fulfilling life. Much of the credit goes to my grandchildren. They keep me excited about life, make me laugh, and inspire me. Instead of me saving them, the twins have saved me from becoming a boring old lady.

WORRY, WORRY, WORRY

Worry comes with the grandparenting territory. You may wonder if you're doing it "right." You may worry about a grandchild repeating family history and choosing a self-defeating path. You may worry about money, especially with the rising cost of food and gas. But the biggest worry may be dying before your grandchildren are prepared for life. There's so much to do and so little time.

Susan Adcox writes about worries in her article, "When Grandparenting Isn't Fun." She thinks grandparents are champion worriers and I agree with her. Worry isn't necessarily a bad thing, according to Adcox, and keeps us on our toes. We must realize and accept the fact that we can't control our children or grandchildren. "The sooner we realize that, the sooner we will be able to take joy in our relationship with them [grandchildren] instead of trying to prevent anything bad from ever happening," she writes.

As the title of her article implies, worry can take the fun out of grandparenting, and it's best to take action before this happens. Joining a support group, seeing a financial advisor, and getting a physical exam are three action steps you can take. Put a damper on worry before it puts a damper on you.

Self-worry is a challenge, as I discovered the year my husband was in Vietnam. He was a hospital commander in the central highlands and I worried about him every day. I also worried about my worry. If I didn't contain my worries they could take over my life. Craft projects were one of my solutions and they took my mind off my worries. My part-time teaching job also helped me put worries aside.

GRIEF AFTER A DEATH

Adults understand the finality of death, yet it remains a mystery. We can only imagine how mysterious death is for children. Never tell children that death is like going to sleep. This comparison can make them afraid of going to bed and afraid they will die. While kids become aware of death when pets die, it takes time to realize a deceased pet, family member, or friend isn't coming back.

Anger is a huge issue for a teen who is grieving because the person who died "really screwed up their life," according to Dr. Heidi Horsley and Dr. Gloria Horsley, authors of *Teen Grief Relief.* The guilt issue can be complicated, and many grieving teens feel guilty for not spending more time with the deceased. Shame arises when friends abandon teens. "Your teenager longs to be popular and envied, not pitied," the Horsleys explain.

Healing Your Grieving Heart for Teens by Alan D. Wolfelt, PhD, contains 100 practical ideas for teens to cope with grief. It's a wide-ranging collection of tips. Here are three of my favorites and some comments about them.

Do something fun. Dedicate it to the one you lost. After our daughter died, all of us needed a break from grief, so we took the twins to Alaska. The two and a half-week trip (cruise and land) was just what we needed. Our grandchildren roamed the ship (I think they checked every nook and cranny), enjoyed the food and entertainment. We laughed together, something we really needed to do, and saw a moose, something my granddaughter wanted to do. Looking back, we realized the trip prepared the twins for living with us.

Do something the person who died liked to do. The twin's father loved fishing and they love it too. Fishing is always on the schedule when we visit relatives in Wisconsin. My granddaughter has a part-time job at a sporting goods store. A customer asked her if she had ever fished. "Yes, she answered." Then he asked if she ever caught a fish and she gave the same answer. When she told me this story my granddaughter said the question was insulting. "He wouldn't ask a male that," she declared. Not only is my granddaughter an excellent fisherwoman, she is her own woman.

Remember the good times. Recovery cannot be rushed. Each of us comes to terms with grief in our own time. Thankfully, the time came when all of us could share stories about deceased loved ones. My granddaughter remembered her mother's meatloaf. "It was awesome," she said. I told her the recipe came from me. "I know," she replied. "But it isn't the same." It would never be the same, I explained, and that was the truth of the matter. Nothing could replace the love and care her mother put into making meatloaf for her children.

CHILDREN'S GRIEF

Children's grief depends on age. Even babies are able to pick up on your tension and sense something is wrong. Brook Noel and Pamela D. Blair, PhD describe children's grief in their book, *I Wasn't Ready to Say Goodbye,* and here's a summary of the basics.

Babies (newborn to 18 months). According to the authors, babies respond to loss and can "feel it in their bones."

Babies show they are upset by fussing, clinging, and wakefulness. You can help by establishing a routine, sticking to it, using soothing words, and giving extra hugs. Using a slider chair and hugging a little one may comfort you and your grandchild.

Toddlers (18 months to three years old). This age group responds to grief with regression, whining, and demands. Though older toddlers and children who are two and three years old have words, they don't have the emotional vocabulary (enough words) to express their feelings. Grandparents can help by setting limits, sticking to them, and answering questions. You may also show them a homemade version of the Wong-Baker Faces Pain Rating Scale, a series of facial expressions available on the Internet. Get three plain paper plates. Draw two eyes, a nose, and a smile on the first. Draw two eyes, a nose, and a straight mouth on the second. Draw two eyes, a nose, and a downturned mouth on the third. Draw a face with tears and a downturned mouth on a fourth. Ask the child to point to the plate or plates that show how he or she is feeling.

Young children (three to 10 years old). Kids start to understand death when they're about five years old. These children fear they will be abandoned and need constant reassurance, according to the authors. You can help by being patient, answering the same questions time and again. Distractions, such as reading to children, baking cookies, and going for a walk may also help.

Teenagers. This is a time of mood changes and peer influence. Today, many schools have support groups for teens. Creative projects also help teens work through their feelings. You may help by giving teenagers privacy and time to process their feelings. Remember, teens are trying to pull away from adults and your probing may look like an attempt to control them.

The American Cancer Society also delves into childhood grief in its website article, "Helping a Child or Teenager Who is Grieving." The article notes that children are unable to process thoughts and emotions as adults do, "so they will need to have many short conversations." You may have to repeat facts often. Children need accurate information, the article says, and you need to use real words like "died." The challenge for grandparents, it seems to me, is to process our own grief while caring for grandchildren. It isn't easy.

UP AND DOWN EMOTIONS

Blending grandchildren and grandparents into a new family is a daunting task. You may think you're doing well and then your grandchildren get into a fight. When you're upset, a grandchild may do something so funny you burst out laughing. Everybody's feelings are going up and down like waves in the sea.

You will survive only if you ignore the small stuff. Messes can be cleaned up. Dirty clothes can wait another day or two. The house won't collapse if you don't dust the furniture. Errands can be postponed. Sometimes you just have to call time out, sit down, and take a well-deserved break.

Jim Fay and Foster W. Cline, MD, offer some tips for coping with up and down emotions in their book, *Grandparenting with Love & Logic*. These tips were written with divorce in mind, yet they apply to other situations. One tip is to avoid criticizing your grandchildren's parents. Criticism doesn't get you anywhere and may put you behind. Not taking sides is a second tip and, while this is easier said than done, at least you can try.

I would add a third tip and that is to praise your grandchildren. A one-sentence compliment can boost a grandchild's self-esteem in seconds. Giving compliments also makes you feel good.

My grandson does things for me, such as taking out the trash and lifting heavy objects, and I always thank him. His reply: "Glad to do it, Grandma." He compliments me as well and his compliments are often about food, such as "Smells Good," or "Looks Good,' or "Thanks, grandma. Dinner was delicious." What are some things you could say?

- You did such a good job of putting your toys away.
- Wow you're funny!
- That color makes your eyes sparkle.
- I like the way you help your baby brother (or sister).
- Good job!
- Thanks for using your inside voice.
- Reading stories to you is so much fun.
- You're a good friend.

THOSE DISTURBING DREAMS

Loss creates stress and stress creates dreams. I've had many dreams about my deceased loved ones, yet remember only a few. Recently I had a dream about searching for my deceased mother and father-in-law. I wanted to tell them how well their great grandchildren were doing and, though I kept searching and searching, couldn't find them. The dream had a sense of urgency. When I awakened I still felt this urgency and then I felt sad.

Maybe I had the dream because my mother and father-in-law never knew the twin's parents died in separate car crashes or that we became GRGs. The dream may be telling me these family members are gone forever. It may also be an indication of pride. At breakfast time the dream was still in my mind and I missed two of the finest people I've ever known. I will always miss them.

Some believe their deceased loved ones contact them through dreams. I'm not one of those people. The human mind is the ultimate computer, and I think dreams are a reflection of the information we're processing. Judy Tatelbaum writes about dreams in her book, *The Courage to Grieve*. She thinks dreams help us re-experience events, work through them, and problem-solve. "Not remembering dreams, even feeling anesthetized through the night, is not unusual during mourning," she explains.

Tatelbaum goes on to say some dreams express our wishes, like my wish to speak with my mother and father-in-law. I've had many dreams about my daughter when she was a baby and toddler. Apparently my mind wants to recall this precious time of life, and these dreams are always in color.

Marty Tousley, a psychiatric nurse for 40 years, discusses dreaming in her article, "Persistent Dreams in Grief," posted on the Open to Hope Foundation website. It's normal to start dreaming six months into grief, Tousley notes, "when all the initial shock and denial have fallen away." Dreaming is the mind's way of coming to terms with reality. If you are troubled by your dreams you may seek help from a physician, grief expert, or health professional trained in Guided Imagery and/or

Imagery Rehearsal Therapy. Keeping a dream journal may also help.

"Grief dreams act as shock-absorbers, help us sort out our emotions, enable us to continue our inner relationship with the deceased, and make a creative bridge to our future," Tousley continues. Don't let disturbing dreams keep you off balance. Think of them as normal, for surely it is normal to dream about the people we loved and continue to love so much.

HOW KIDS EXPRESS THEIR FEELINGS

Babies express their feelings with fussy behavior, crying and head-banging. Toddlers express their feelings with tantrums and regressive behavior. Preschoolers may express their feelings with magical thinking and story-telling. Years ago, when I was still teaching, one of my students told me a story about a man who decided to raise chickens. When chickens wandered away he didn't try to find them. The boy continued to tell the story, adding details and "chapters." I realized he was talking about his father, who was a health care professional, not a chicken farmer. Story-telling helped this little boy to release pent-up feelings.

Alan J. Wolfelt, PhD, shares many ways kids can express themselves in his book, *Healing Your Grieving Heart for Teens.* His suggestions range from keeping a journal, to lighting candles, to reversing roles, to art projects. Observe your grandchildren closely and you will discover the ways they express themselves.

One of the most successful art activities I ever came up with were comics pages. I gave nursery school students drawing paper with dialogue balloons on them (like the ones in the comics), only the balloons were blank. Some dialogue balloons were at the top, some were in the middle, and some were at the bottom. I asked the kids to draw pictures about how they were feeling that day. After they finished the pictures, the kids dictated the dialogue, and I wrote it in the balloons.

The results were amazing, and the kids kept asking for more comics pages. Several arranged their pictures on the table like real comics. You can choose different themes for the comics: family pets, favorite toys, best friends, or family members. Your grandchildren could even make a comic book about living with grandma and grandpa. Comics pages may even become an ongoing project.

YOUR OLD NORMAL AND NEW NORMAL

"New normal" has become a common term and is used to describe temperature changes, business plans, community changes, and more. According to an online medical dictionary, the term refers to changes "after a traumatic loss of a loved one." I think the term also applies to grandparents who are raising their grandchildren. You had an old life and are now living a new one.

Before, in your old life, you had more freedom. Today, you have less freedom and more challenges. How you define your new normal depends, in part, on the ages of your grandchildren. If you're caring for infants this life includes bottle feeding, diaper changing, and bathing wiggling bodies. If you're caring for toddlers chances are you're running all the time and dealing with "No!" If you're caring for preschoolers you're answering questions and planning all sorts of activities. If you're caring for grade school children you are helping with homework, attending parent conferences, school plays and concerts.

Teenagers are a different story altogether. For one thing, teens turn to their peers first, via emails, text messaging, Facebook, Skype, and phone calls. Like most teenagers, my grandchildren check their cell phones constantly and use them to take photos, get driving directions, and find out about events. I have basic cell phone service and use it for emergency calls only. The twins think I'm old-fashioned, whereas I think I'm practical.

Adjusting to your new normal takes effort because the timing is off. Just as you were about to slow down, life made you go faster. This fact, alone, is frustrating. You need emotional support for yourself and the children in your care. A child with a personality disorder, who has been physically or emotionally abused, is a special challenge. No doubt about it, you have your work cut out for you. Maybe you don't even want to think about what is ahead.

D IS FOR DENIAL

You may be so busy with daily tasks that you don't see the grief in your life. Still, it's there, lingering in the back of your mind. Bob Deits discusses denial in his book, *Life After Loss.* According to Deits, denial can happen without us being aware of it, and this may have happened to you. Thoughts about child care may block other thoughts from your mind.

After the initial "Oh no!" reaction you may slip into denial. This is normal after a loss, according to Deits. The important thing is to recognize denial and deal with it. Take a good look at your grandchild or grandchildren. Has troubling behavior become harmful? Is one grandchild more aggressive than another? Do your grandchildren play fairly? Has a teenager used scary words?

Delayed treatment, even death, can be the consequences of denial. This isn't the time for denial. You need to watch for symptoms that may indicate a serious physical or mental health problem. Instincts are an early-warning system and you need to trust them. If your instincts tell you a grandchild has a serious problem, heed this instinct and get help immediately. It's better to be safe than sorry.

Members of the extended family may be in denial, as many blog posts indicate. A post on the Daily Strength Blog describes the steps two parents took to save their addicted daughter. "We tried everything, and I mean everything. Rehab. AA. Church. Endless meetings at school. Spending more time with her. Spending less time with her. This, that, counseling." Nothing worked, the mother wrote, and her 16-year-old daughter ran away.

Now the couple is raising their granddaughter. But family members criticized the couple's parenting and said they didn't do enough. One couple took the addicted daughter into their home, only to throw her out a month later. Years later, family members apologized to these GRGs for their enabling. Your story may be similar, so be aware of denial because it's far-reaching.

CHOOSING HAPPINESS

Americans have the right to pursue happiness, yet many of us fail to find it. Some of us don't find it because we're overwhelmed and stressed. Yet in the earliest days of my grandparenting journey I realized I was blessed. I love children of all ages, love being with them, and this works in my favor. Having an even, upbeat personality works in my favor as well.

Happiness starts with the decision to view life through bright lenses instead of dark. Let me give you an example of this vision. Years ago, my husband and I attended a medical conference. We met friends we had known for years and decided to visit the local sights with them. When the husband got into the car, he was grumpy and out of sorts. But when his wife got into the car, she was smiling and eager. The husband made a negative comment and the wife replied, "I don't know about you, but I'm going to have a wonderful day." Her comment changed the husband's attitude instantly.

"Me too," he replied with a grin.

Tom Valeo writes about the happiness choice in his WebMD article, "Strategies for Happiness: 7 Steps to Becoming a Happy Person." The first step is the decision I just mentioned. Other steps, gratitude, forgiveness, positive thinking, friendship, and meaningful activities, are things you've thought about, but may not have knit together. "Remember, money can't buy happiness," Valeo advises.

One of the best things I've learned is how to balance negative thoughts with positive ones. I've been doing this for years. When a negative thought enters my mind, I think of a positive one. Developing this skill takes practice but, thankfully, I've learned to do it. In fact, I've done it so long it is automatic. Dr. Heidi Horsley and Dr. Gloria Horsley call this process "thought stopping," and it's a good term. Positive thinking changed my life and it can change yours. Each morning, as you tumble out of bed, tell yourself, "I'll find something to be happy about today." And you will.

Positive thinking helped me choose happiness over sadness. I had been sad too long and it was time to be happy again. You can make the same choice. Maybe it's time to leave sadness behind and enjoy the happiness you deserve. Like rain, happiness comes in little drops, the drops accumulate, and eventually you have a puddle of happiness, or even a lake. Each day, you may choose happiness over sadness.

WHAT WORKS

- Recognize and accept the grief in your life.
- Watch for signs of children's grief.
- Use a simplified version of the faces rating scale.
- Praise your grandchildren.
- Ask your grandchildren to create comics pages about their feelings.
- Practice "thought stopping."
- Find something to be happy about each day.

3

NEW LIFE, NEW RESPONSIBILITIES

Just because you're living a new life doesn't mean you can't enjoy it. Seeing children grow adds humor, zest and wonder to our lives. Years ago I participated in a televised panel discussion about parenting. At the end of the discussion, one panelist commented on her children's younger years. "I have three children, but when they were young I was so busy with work I didn't have time to enjoy them," she said. What a sad admission.

Enjoying our grandchildren should come first, in my opinion, and that should be the basis of all caregiving. You may have to rearrange furniture, buy some things, or even do some construction to meet your grandchildren's needs. After the construction messes are cleaned up your grandchildren will be grateful.

BEGIN WITH THE BASICS

Basic needs include nutritious food, appropriate clothing, shelter that is warm and dry, clean air, opportunities to exercise, an education, a safe environment (including safety rules), medical and dental care. Love is the starting point in meeting these needs. Tell your grandchildren you love them as often as possible. Hugs are important, too. Teens may feel like you're invading personal space if you hug them or be embarrassed by this gesture. So you'll have to be sensitive to the time, the place, and others are present. Before I hug my grandchildren I ask for their permission.

Adults appreciate a cozy bed and so do grandchildren. See if you can arrange for the children to sleep in their same beds. We hired a moving van and moved our daughter's bedroom furniture from their vacant home to our home. My grandson sleeps in his mother's bed and uses her desk. My granddaughter sleeps in her mother's childhood bed and uses her antique dresser. Though the twins never said anything, I think sleeping in their mother's beds is a source of comfort.

Children have other needs as well. Meredith Laden writes about them in her article, "Understand The Five Essentials Children Need from Parents." She lists the needs: acceptance, affection, attention, affirmation, and accountability. But parents and grandparents aren't perfect, and Meredith thinks "parents teach that mistakes are a learning experience and not necessarily a bad thing."

Before you became a GRG or GAP your grandchildren may have been neglected. Indeed, you may have witnessed the neglect and been heartbroken by it. As you care for your grandchildren you not only have to make them feel loved and secure, you have to counter the consequences of neglect. This is one instance where patience pays off.

Keeping my grandchildren safe was a priority for us. The safety issue became more important when my grandson asked if he could sleep under a bridge with his friends. I'm originally from Long Island, New York, where anyone who sleeps under a bridge is homeless, mentally ill, or running from the law. Sleeping under a bridge isn't my idea of recreation. While we understood our grandson's need for adventure, his request made us nervous, and we contacted a friend's mother. She asked us to come over to discuss the issue.

After we had been chatting a while she said, "Just a minute. I know the county sheriff and I'm going to call her." According to the sheriff, sleeping under the bridge was safe mid-week and unsafe on weekends, when vagrants camped there. She agreed to check on the boys. This eased our worries, and we also drove to the site and inspected it. Evidence of previous campers, gathered twigs and a cleared sleeping area, were still there.

Since our grandson and his buddies were all experienced campers, we let him sleep under the bridge. The guys cooked hot dogs over a fire, snuggled in sleeping bags near the stream, and had a great time. We slept better knowing the sheriff was on watch. I can't say we slept well, however.

YOU AREN'T REPLACING PARENTS

Moving is one of the most stressful experiences of life. Children who are forced to move may become resentful. We knew we could never replace the twin's parents and we wouldn't even try. Communicating with teens can be tricky, but I took a chance anyway. "I hope you know we aren't trying to replace your parents," I told my granddaughter. "We're your grandparents and always will be."

She nodded her head in agreement. In the years they have lived with us, I think the twins have realized we love each other, have a close relationship, are honest, keep our promises, and want the best for them.

Keep assuring your grandchildren that you're not trying to replace their parents. Older children will figure this out by observing your actions and decisions. Younger children will need to hear this message many times before they understand it. End the conversation with a reassuring sentence such as, "Being your Grandpa is so much fun."

Still, things may not go well, according to "Grandparents Raising Grandchildren: A Call to Action," a Head Start Report prepared by Deborah M. Whitley, PhD, and Susan J. Kelly, PhD. Whitley is the Director of the National Center on Grandparents Raising Grandchildren at Georgia State University. There is little research on how children are coping with living with their grandparents. Early trauma can have long-lasting effects on children. Some youngsters may have thinking problems, poor motor skills, poor eye-hand coordination, social and emotional delays. Teenage grandchildren may respond by being anti-social and acting out. "Emotions such as anger and frustration due to feelings of abandonment, parental confusion, and attachment disorder may be manifested in early sexual activity, gang activity, drug use, poor school performance, and violent behavior toward peers and/or family members," the authors observe.

In situations like these early intervention is crucial. In fact, it can turn things around. Get professional help for your grandchildren if they are combative and think you're trying to replace their parents after living with you for months. Take action before a bad situation becomes worse.

IDENTIFYING RESPONSIBILITES AND TASKS

Becoming a GRG or GAP is a role that takes practice. You don't suddenly jump on the grandparenting stage, know your lines, and say them convincingly. As you practice your new role it becomes clearer to you. The gymnastics banquet is a good example. I knew I was supposed to bring food to share, but my granddaughter forgot to tell me that I was supposed to bring plates, cups and utensils. Fortunately, another couple had brought extras and gave them to us. You can bet I brought everything the next year.

Just as roots spread out from a tree, tasks spread out from responsibilities. You may wind up with far more tasks than anticipated. Since I'm a visual person I made a chart of my responsibilities and tasks. Though each responsibility is followed by three example tasks, there are actually many more. See chart on next page.

Responsibilities and tasks are all about adaptation. You're adapting to a new situation and so are your grandkids. The University of Florida, in a website article titled "Grandparents Raising Grandchildren: Building Strong Families," says adaptation takes practice. Whether you're ready for it or not, adaptation also takes compromise. You should always ask, "What's best for my grandchildren?" Use this test question again and again.

RESPONSIBILITIES AND TASKS CHART

Responsibility: Fix balanced, nutritious meals.

Frequent trips to the grocery store
Making dishes from scratch
Giving grandchildren food choices

Responsibility: Provide a comfortable, cozy home.

Painting bedroom walls
Hiring a moving van to move furniture to our home
Replacing old carpet with wood flooring

Responsibility: Provide and/or arrange for medical and dental care.

Arranging for twins to see our dentist
Using father's medical/dental insurance
Arranging for counseling

Responsibility: Provide transportation.

Taxi service when needed
Loaning my car to the twins
Keeping my car gas tank full

AGE-APPROPRIATE CAREGIVING

As you make your way through the caregiving maze, you have to consider your grandchildren's ages and stages. The food you prepare, the schedule you set, and the toys you buy should match the age of each child. But I'm worried about today's children. Unstructured play seems to be disappearing and we can't let that happen.

Many children have over-structured lives and race from one activity to the next. Too many are spending their time staring at television and text messaging. In fact, text messaging has led to health problems, children with arthritic thumbs and sore necks from hunching over computer screens. Technology is wonderful, no doubt about it, but children need free time and physical activity.

Basic play materials, a sand box and sand toys, wooden building blocks, and water play, are still some of the best activities for young children. Children all over the world gravitate to these things. I was reminded of this as my husband and I walked along a city street and saw three young children playing in a sand pile. The sand had been piled up for a nearby construction project and the kids couldn't resist it. They picked up sand in their hands and watched it trickle to the ground. They tried to model the sand and, though it wasn't wet enough, they kept trying.

Watching the children play with sand made me think of my own childhood. I grew up in safe times and my brother and I roamed the neighborhood. In the summer, we played kick the can for hours and caught fireflies in jelly jars. We went sailing on Long Island Sound in my brother's small boat or went swimming at Jones Beach on Long Island. Nobody in the neighborhood had television then. We finally bought one when I was a high school senior. In the evening, people sat on their front porches, chatted about the day, and waited for the ice cream truck.

In the winter, we played board games, Canasta, and read books by the dozen. We can't bring this innocent time back, but we can provide sand, blocks, and water play for youngsters. Instead of over-scheduling them we can let them play, one of the most important components of childhood. While children are playing they're also problem-solving and dreaming. Maybe it has been years since you were in the company of young children. To refresh your mind you may wish to take out some child development books from the library.

One last reminder. Middle and high school children may be "techies" but they also like things that remind them of childhood, a stuffed animal, mini Frisbee, or puzzle. Be on the lookout for these things because they're wonderful stocking stuffers and birthday gifts.

SETTING NEW GOALS

It's hard to think about goals when you're a new GRG or GAP. My goal was to make it to the next hour and work up to a day. When I could function almost normally for a day, I changed my goal to a week. When I could function almost normally for a week, I changed my goal to a month. Goals change with the passage of time. Robert D. Strom and Shirley K. Strom, of Arizona State University in Tempe, write about goals in their research paper, "Meeting the Challenge of Raising Grandchildren."

Grandparents who are raising their grandchildren have common goals, according to the Stroms. First, these grandparents know they will have to revise personal goals to fit their current situation. Second, they know childhood has changed since they raised their kids. Third, GRGs may have to cooperate with the parent who shares responsibility for the child. Fourth, children's growth and academic performance need to be monitored. Fifth, grandparents in the caregiving trenches need a break every so often.

When we set new goals we have to remain optimistic. But the Stroms think middle-income Caucasians often resist this goal. "Their opposition comes from the belief that caring for a grandchild requires a loss of their freedom," they write. Sadly, grandchildren who sense this feeling may feel unwanted.

Young children, even infants, can pick up on an optimistic attitude. In the long run, optimism will help your grandchildren. As the Stroms explain, "Research shows that optimists do better academically, in athletics, and at the workplace because they cheerfully persist when confronted with setbacks." So you may wish to make optimism your first goal. Looking on the bright side will energize you and make your days easier.

No matter how old we are we still have goals. Setting new goals is a way of taking care of yourself. One of my goals is to keep writing books, for example. Start simply if you haven't set new goals in a while. Writing goals on paper may make them seem more real to you.

You may promise to yourself that you will relax for at least a half hour each day. Trying a new hobby may be a new goal. Or you may wish to become better at the hobby you already have and decide to become an expert wood carver or fly fisherperson. Another goal may be to reactivate friendships that have fallen by the wayside. Goal-setting keeps you involved in life and that's good.

LEGAL HELP

Our daughter had listed us as the twin's guardians in her will. Even with this declaration, we knew we needed legal help. We sought help from the lawyer who had drawn up the will and had known our daughter. She grasped our situation immediately. Without her help, I don't think we would have been able to navigate the legal system as easily.

Many grandparents need legal help in order to keep a child from being taken from a home or to get legal custody of him or her. You may be one of them. The problem is, you may not know the types of custody that exist. "Too often, grandparents do not have a legal relationship with their grandchildren, largely due to the informal way in which they obtained responsibility for their grandchildren," Deborah M. Whitley, PhD, and Susan J. Kelly, PhD, explain in their report, "Grandparents Raising Grandchildren: A Call to Action."

As we navigated the legal system, we were increasingly grateful to our daughter for having a will. Though our case didn't come on the court docket for months, when we went to court with our lawyer, guardianship and conservatorship were granted quickly. Legal arrangements vary from state to state and you may need to hire a lawyer to help you understand these arrangements.

In some cases, grandparents petition the court for legal custody because the parents are unfit. Grandchildren may be put in what's called legal foster care, an arrangement for a child or children to live with relatives or grandparents.

Adoption is also an option. Under this arrangement the parental rights are terminated and grandparents are legally and finally responsible for grandchildren.

Becoming a guardian or conservator requires endless paperwork. My husband, bless him, was in charge of this paperwork, and filling out one form could take days. The county court required detailed proof of how we spent the grandchildren's inheritance, their Social Security funds, and the money in the twin's bank accounts. Despite the work involved, we think documentation is a good thing because it prevents adults from taking money from minors.

Our guardianship and conservatorship were rescinded shortly after the twins turned 18, yet we are still involved in their lives. In fact, we call them "our kids" because that's what they are and we are blessed.

FULFILLING LEGAL OBLIGATIONS

Start a file of legal documents regarding your grandchildren. This file may include birth certificates, death certificates, receipts, and other documents. Visit the local Social Security office if you have questions about the benefits your grandchildren are entitled to and the paperwork that supports these benefits. A staff person will be able to save you hours of work and worry.

Our legal obligations were so extensive we kept the lawyer who had helped us previously. She guided us through many situations and was always in court with us. Going to court the first time was an emotional experience. Our case was third on the court docket and I listened to the previous cases. One woman started to cry, pulled herself together, and said, "Thank you for giving me the money to feed my children." I wanted to cry with her. Another case involved a demented man represented by legal counsel. He lived in a nursing home and the judge called him on a speaker phone. When the judge asked the man questions, he was silent, so the judge terminated the call. "Thank you for talking with us," the judge said. I wanted to cry for that man too.

Your financial situation may be so dire that you are unable to fulfill your obligations; in that case turn to the national or state government for help. Laura T. Coffey, in her "Today" show article, "10 Tips for Grandparents Raising Grandchildren," says you should examine your legal status and determine your eligibility for this help. "An easy way to see what government support might exist for you is to fill out a confidential questionnaire at www.BenefitsCheckUp.org," she advises.

Other thorny questions may arise. Who owns the car that's parked in a parent's garage? Can your grandchildren inherit it? Do the items in a vacated house belong to parents or your grandchildren? Fulfilling legal obligations is a time-consuming process. You do it for yourself and the next generation.

FINANCIAL AID

You may have to act like a detective to get financial assistance. Grandparent-headed families are usually eligible for food stamps and Medicaid. "Grandparents are not fully aware that they too are eligible for certain services and benefits," according to Whitley and Kelly.

For example you may be eligible for monthly benefits to help with child care. In Region IV of the US, which includes

Alabama, Florida, Georgia, Kentucky, Mississippi, North and South Carolina, and Tennessee, grandparents may be eligible for CRISP Payments, Emergency/Crisis Intervention Services.

The Administration for Children and Families, part of the US Department of Health and Human Services, provides additional funds for GRGs and GAPs. These funds are Temporary Assistance for Needy Families, Child Care and Development Fund, Child Support Enforcement, Child Welfare, Developmental Disabilities, and Head Start. Whitley and Kelly recommend a coordinated service system "that promotes strong and stable families." For more help contact the National Center for Grandparents Raising Grandchildren. Their mailing address is Georgia State University, 140 Decatur Street, Urban Life Building, Suite 1248, Atlanta, Georgia 30303.

In addition to national and state aid, local agencies and churches may have funds available. We went to the local Social Security office and asked for more information. A staff person told us how the money could be spent and we followed his advice. This made record-keeping easier and made it easier for my husband to complete the paperwork. Our grandchildren inherited some money and needed to keep good records, so I bought portable file boxes for them.

Filing taxes may be a worry for you. The Grandparents Weekly website has posted some tips for you, "Tax Tips for Grandparents Raising Grandchildren." The article says the Internal Revenue service will give you a tax break "just for having a child living in your home." Federal credit programs, the Earned Income Tax Credit, Child Tax Credit, and Child and Dependent Care Tax Credit, are also available. "Tax credits are better than tax deductions because you can subtract a tax credit from any federal income tax that you owe," the article explains, "whereas a deduction only reduces the income that you used to figure out the taxes you owe." Contact your State Department of Revenue or an income tax service for more tips.

You may also contact the Administration for Children and Families (ACF) which is part of the US Department of Health and Human Services. This department oversees several programs that may help you: Temporary Assistance to Needy Families, Child Care and Development Fund, Child Welfare, Child Support and Enforcement, and Developmental Disabilities.

PARENT VISITS

A visiting parent may cause some problems. Since grandchildren may be excited and worried at the same time, it's best to prepare for these visits. Diane Bales, an Extension Human Development Specialist, summarizes points from several resources in her University of Georgia website article, "Grandparents Raising Grandchildren: Helping Grandchildren Stay in Contact With Parents." She offers these tips for smooth visits. I've changed the wording and added some comments.

1. **Be flexible with schedules.** Your plans may change and the parent's plans may change. When you make plans, it's a good idea to make a contingency plan. Try and have visits on a certain day of the week and at a certain time. List the visits on the calendar. Put stickers on these dates so young children can keep track of them.

2. **Treat parent or parents with respect.** Despite the mixed feelings you have, keep them under control. Be courteous and, if you can, let the parent do most of the talking. You may wish to end the visit with a funny story about the grandchildren. Ending a visit with laughter sets the stage for other successful visits.

3. **Keep communication lines open.** Visits are stressful and you may wish to make a list of talking points and practice them aloud. Because a high voice can be an indication of stress, keep your voice low and calm. Talk about the children's school achievements, their new friends, and share any new contact information you may have, such as a cell phone number.

4. **Be respectful of grandchildren's feelings.** Visits arouse conflicting feelings in grandchildren, happiness at seeing their parent and sadness when they recall bad memories. "Don't make children feel guilty about enjoying the time they spend with their parent," Bales advises. Though you may not feel it, try to act happy about each visit.

5. **Strive for normal.** Deep in your heart, you know life isn't normal, but you can still make the visits seem that way. Offer the parent a snack. Share news, things like a grandson learning to ride a two-wheeler, a granddaughter with a new haircut. Playing games together may also foster normalcy. The parent may also read a story to his or her child.

6. **Be consistent.** Share your house rules with the parent before he or she comes to visit. According to Bales, grandparents should expect some deviation from these rules during the first visits. If this happens, remind the parent of the rules and that rules are for your grandchild's safety

and wellbeing. Everyone is feeling their way, and this is a time for patience.

7. **Be alert to stress.** Signs of stress include complaints about stomachaches, headaches, and muscle aches. Your grandchildren's behavior may regress and the children may argue among themselves or with you. Keep your cool and reassure children with hugs and calming activities, such as baking cookies together.

8. **Give grandchildren control.** Ask your grandchildren to choose some activities to enjoy during the visit. You and your grandchildren may also plan some things to talk about. Grandchildren may also help by gathering items – games, favorite books, a football or Frisbee. Your grandchildren may even plan what they want to wear.

Sadly, some parents are a no-show. The only thing you can do is tell your grandchildren the truth in age-appropriate words. You may refer to future visits, but don't build them up too much. A parent may be unable to visit because he or she is in prison, hospitalized, or undergoing drug treatment. To stay in touch, grandchildren may send the parent letters, drawings, photos, emails, or call them on the phone. "Help them adjust to this change in their lives by being there listening to feelings, and letting them know you love them," Bales advises.

Travel may also present a problem. Get passports early if you plan to travel to another country with your grandchildren. A local travel agency arranged for our trip to Alaska. To be on the safe side, the agent asked us to get a permission letter from the twin's father, who was living with them at that time. Customs agents never asked us about our grandchildren, but we were still glad we had the letter.

WHY TEENS ARE DIFFERENT

Several factors make teens different from younger children. One of the most important differences is their feeling of invincibility and a "nothing will happen to me" attitude. "You worry too much, Grandma," my granddaughter said. I told her life made me a worrier. You can present facts, review plans, cite dangers, list potential consequences, and teens will still think they're invincible.

Teens turn to their peers first for support. This is okay if they receive it, but when peer group members stop calling and texting, life is bleak for teens. Another factor complicates caregiving and it's the teenagers' tendency to look and act strong when they're really falling apart inside. This is hard on you and them. Privacy is another issue and it's a biggie. Teenagers want their own space and your probing may look like interference.

The human brain isn't fully developed until age 25 and you need to remember this. You're dealing with an immature brain and talking won't change this. Pleading won't change this. Threatening won't change this. Punishment won't change this. Indeed, teenagers will simply turn you off, tune you out, and do what they want. That's why communication skills, the subject of the next chapter, are so important.

Grandparents who are caring for grandkids need to take a deep breath and "go with the flow." Time is on our side, and teenagers that have acted immature this week may do something unbelievably mature the next. Eventually this up and down behavior levels out, something I realized at the twin's high school graduations. "When did they become so grown up?" I asked myself. I asked myself this question again during their first college break, at Thanksgiving and Christmas. Every time they come home from college I ask myself this question. The twins are young adults, yet I still think of them as kids.

BE READY FOR CHANGE

Becoming GRGs changed our lives and some of the changes were boggling. For some time, we had wanted to replace our upstairs carpet with wood flooring. Hectic as our lives were, we proceeded with these plans. Eddie, our flooring expert and a true craftsman, laid the wood, hung a plastic vapor barrier from the ceiling, and started varnishing. Even with the barrier, the smell was so strong we went to the movies to escape it. Our grandson went down to the basement to watch television.

When we returned from the movies, Eddie was sitting in his truck in front of the driveway. He looked pale and worried. "Something's wrong," I said to my husband, as we pulled alongside.

"Which do you want first, good news or the bad?" Eddie asked. I opted for the former. "The good news is that I have insurance," he began. "The bad news is that I tripped and spilled a can of varnish down your stairs." We went inside to assess the damage. Eddie had spilled an industrial-size can of varnish and every step was blotched with it. Our newly painted walls were splashed with varnish as well. This was going to be one heck of a clean-up job.

"What happened?" I asked, and he recounted the story. Apparently my grandson was using his cell phone and accidentally hit the panic button several times. We have a security system and the signal went straight to police headquarters. Minutes later, a police car parked in front of the house and two officers emerged with drawn guns. They rang the doorbell, which plays "There's No Place Like Home," a song so obnoxious it's a wonder they didn't shoot the bell. (It came with the house, but re-programming instructions didn't.)

Entering the front door, the police saw the main level was a wreck, filled with furniture, shelves, books, and lamps. Fearing foul play, they went upstairs, guns still drawn, approached Eddie from behind, and scared him out of his wits. "I saw their shadows first," he explained, "turned around and saw the police and the guns." After they realized nothing was wrong upstairs, the officers decided to check the basement, and opened the door just as my grandson reached the top step. He was shocked to see the police. "What's happening?" he asked. Later, our grandson told us he had heard "too many footsteps" above him and went upstairs to investigate. Everything was straightened out and the officers left. A week later we received a stern letter from the police department, saying if this happened again we would be fined $350.

Processing Eddie's insurance claim took weeks. Finally, a check arrived and we could proceed. New carpeting was installed and the walls were re-painted. "We just went to the movies," I whined. The moral of this GRG story is that you need to be ready for change, as ready as an Olympic athlete. The "Guns Drawn" story has become part of family lore. You probably have many stories to tell as well, stories that weren't funny at first and you laugh about now.

WHAT WORKS

- Start with the basics.
- Tell your grandchildren you're not replacing their parents.
- Chart your responsibilities and tasks.
- Set personal goals and keep setting them.
- Get legal help if you need it.
- Plan for parent visits.
- Be ready for change.

4

COMMUNICATING WITH KIDS: HELLO?

Communication fascinates me and I've studied it for years. I try to apply what I learn. Ever since the twins moved in with us I've worked hard on communication. From the get-go, I knew I had to keep my sentences short. Good communication is like a phone with a clear outgoing signal and working receiver. Your conversational style also affects reception.

Speech expert Deborah Tannen, PhD, explains different conversational styles in her book, *That's Not What I Meant!* These differences "are analogous to having the wiring in the wrong place," she writes. When participants realize the conversation isn't working, they unintentionally provoke one another, and these actions lead to offending behavior. "As a result, rather than getting more similar, they [conversationalists] get more and more different."

THE POWER OF A CALM VOICE

In the Chinese language pitch changes the meaning of a word. Pitch can also change the meaning of a word or sentence in the English language. Ending a sentence on a high pitch turns it into a question. Tannen thinks pitch is an indication of our attitude and emotional involvement. When you're upset your voice gets higher, something grandchildren notice right away. So even if you're upset, try to speak in a calm voice.

A calm voice can be more powerful than a loud one. Grandkids learn a lot about you by listening to the pitch of your voice and the words you say. After I dropped a juice glass on the kitchen floor there were chards everywhere, under the table, along the wall, and by the kitchen sink. I couldn't understand how a little glass could make such a big mess. "This is terrific," I said in a low, annoyed voice. "Just terrific." I picked up the large pieces and swept the remaining bits of glass into a dust pan. My granddaughter, who was sitting at the kitchen table, watched my clean-up efforts.

"You're funny when you're angry," she said. Her comment was surprising and also showed how closely she observed me.

The next time you're in a difficult situation, try a calm voice. Experienced speakers do this all the time to emphasize points. Your grandchildren are your audience. A calm voice is less threatening and can prevent small problems from becoming big ones. Deep inside your grandchild may be thinking, "I'm so glad grandma (or grandpa) isn't yelling at me. I've heard too much yelling already."

I learned the power of a calm voice during my first year of teaching. Actually, it was the power of a whisper. In the winter I caught a terrible cold and developed laryngitis. Days after the cold was gone I still couldn't talk. Since I had used all of my sick leave, I returned to teaching, though I feared my lack of voice would lead to a chaotic classroom. But my kindergarten students, 40 in the morning and 40 in the afternoon, a staggering total of 80 (illegal today) were fascinated by my whispers. They whispered back and the classroom became quieter and quieter. I think it was the quietest classroom in the school. The whispering experiment taught me that you don't need to be loud to be heard. You just need to care.

VALUES OF SHORT MESSAGES

Children receive short messages more quickly than long ones. But grandparents can be wordy. My husband's stories tend to have long introductions. At dinner one evening he began a story with details from his childhood, details that were interesting to him and less interesting to the twins. Though he was diverted by memories, the twins listened patiently and waited for the plot to develop. It didn't.

I lost my patience and blurted, "Cut to the chase!" This was a rude comment, and later I was sorry I said it, but I couldn't help myself. The twins gave each other "the look," smiled, and resumed eating.

Long messages are often ineffective ones. Robert Bolton, PhD, author of **People Skills**, says this kind of communication has far-reaching effects. "Ineffective communication causes an interpersonal gap that is experienced in all facets of life and in all sectors of society," he writes. Family problems and loneliness are part of this gap. As Bolton explains, "The most intense loneliness today is often found in the family where communication is breaking down or in shambles."

You and I don't want loneliness for our grandchildren. We want them to feel like part of the family – secure, comfortable, cherished and loved. The next time you have a conversation with your grandchildren, use short sentences. If you aren't able to make all of your points, you have the option of continuing the conversation at a later time.

Thinking of conversations as emails may help you. Many websites start conversations that continue for weeks and the topics are called "threads." You can start a thread with young children and stitch it into future conversations. Repeating the stitches will help your grandchildren receive and recall messages.

COMPLIMENTING YOUR GRANDKIDS

Complimenting grandkids can be tricky. When should I do it? What should I say? Where should I say it? Which words should I use? Do I compliment efforts or results? Instead of worrying about my grandparenting style I focus on love. You and I have so much love to give to our grandchildren, and giving compliments is a way to show our love.

In an earlier chapter I listed some one-sentence compliments. They work well because kids remember them. When your grandchildren's friends visit you may compliment them on their clothing or hairstyle, or say "I'm so glad to see you again."

An article on the Family Education website, "Perfecting the Art of the Compliment," makes a distinction between compliments and flattery. Flattery is insincere and excessive, the article notes, whereas real compliments are always sincere. According to the article, the basics of a good compliment are sincerity, specificity, unqualified, and no comparisons. A comparison can totally ruin a compliment. For example, "You did pretty well on today's test, but you really did well on last week's test." Who needs a half-hearted compliment like this?

"How to Give and Receive Compliments," an article on the Teach Kids How website, asks adults to keep these points in mind when giving compliments.

1. Children who receive compliments eventually learn to say "Thank you."
2. We should never ask a child to thank us for a compliment.
3. Shyness keeps some youngsters from responding to compliments.

"A true compliment comes from the giver's heart and impacts the giver's heart," the article summarizes. However, GRGs and GAPs need to keep in mind that excessive compliments may come across as smarmy and grandchildren may think they're being manipulated. After you've complimented your grandchildren, it's best to leave it alone and not add to it. For example, the mother of one of my nursery school students told her son she loved his painting. Then she asked, "What is it?" These three little words negated her compliment instantly.

Finding time to compliment teens can be a challenge because they're so busy with school, after-school activities, and their friends. Instead of giving a verbal compliment, you can give your grandchild a written one. Write your one-sentence compliment on a sticky note and put it on your grandchild's bedroom door. Praise shouldn't be overdone, but keep the statements coming. Your sticky notes may be saved for years to come.

CONSISTENCY COUNTS

This is a confusing time in your grandchildren's lives. Not following house rules adds to their confusion. Your grandchildren need consistency. Dr. Bonnie Zucker cites the values of consistency in her Parents Ask website article, "Parents are Asking: Why is Consistency Important?" She describes consistency as a gift we give to children, in our case, grandchildren. As grandchildren grow and mature, consistency helps them to feel self-confident.

"A lack of consistency can often make children insecure and even chaotic," she comments. I think this comment applies to all children, from babies to teenagers.

Christine Frank also addresses the issue in her Parenting website article "The Need for Parenting Consistency." She advises parents (and grandparents) to pick their battles. "It's our call which issues are worth fighting for." These authors are looking at consistency from a discipline standpoint, but you need language consistency as well. Certain words, especially with teenagers, should not be allowed, and we also need to foster good manners.

My husband and I respect each other and there's no name calling or ridicule in our home. Before we make any plans we check with each other and the twins. All plans are supposed to be on the master calendar, an essential form of communication. "If it isn't on the calendar, it isn't in my mind," I often say. Consistency doesn't mean rigidity. We're willing to adapt to changing circumstances and alter our course when necessary.

Linda Dannison, PhD, and Andrea B. Smith, PhD, contributors to the Family Information Services website, think consistency helps to nurture children. "Providing predictability [or consistency] within the home environment will help increase the children's feelings of security and personal worth." I think our consistency helped the twins in more ways than we know.

TEENAGERS: NO PRYING PLEASE

Pre-teens and teenagers want their "space," another word for privacy, and that means no prying from grandparents. Though you're worried and anxious, you need to refrain from prying and keep your worries to yourself. A WebMD article, "Grief: Helping Teens with Grief," says parents (or grandparents) shouldn't force a teenager to talk about feelings. "If the teen feels comfortable with you and feels that you are willing to listen, he or she will talk when ready."

As you get to know your grandchildren better, you may ask for more facts. "Who are you going to the movies with?" "When does the movie start?" "When will you be home?"

While you don't want to pry, you need basic information. Grandparents are supposed to keep grandchildren safe and your worries stem from safety concerns. Calling friends' parents will help you get the information you need. Still, grandchildren may not accept that you're in charge. Again, it's important to set family rules, abide by them, and ensure children abide by them.

Many child life experts think the computer should be in a high traffic area of your home, such as the kitchen, where you can see the websites children are accessing and what they're doing. Our grandchildren were used to having their computers in their rooms and we continued this practice. Maybe were naive, but we trusted them. We cautioned them, however, about sharing too much personal information on Facebook.

Child life experts also think children shouldn't have dorm refrigerators in their rooms. This is because children who have food on hand tend to become isolated. While you don't want to pry, you may follow these suggestions to monitor your grandchildren. Log into Facebook and look for postings. Ask a tech-savvy colleague or friend to help you if you don't know how to log into Facebook.

Getting to know some of the parents of your grandchildren's friends will help you keep track of things. After our daughter died, a group of parents from her church gave us a list of friends' names, addresses and phone numbers. Their thoughtfulness helped us immensely and was also touching. The next year we received a high school directory with all of the students' names and contact information.

KEEP IT KIND

Never underestimate the value of kindness, for a little kindness goes a long way. Indeed, it will stay in your grandchildren's minds for years. Kindness is reassuring and says, "My grandparents love and care about me." Millie Ferrer-Chancy, Larry F. Forthun and Angela Falcone write about kindness in their website article, "Grandparents Raising Grandchildren: Building Strong Families." They think kindness has an impact on communication.

"Nothing destroys communication faster than the use of unkind words," they write. "When you use unkind words, people tend not to listen to you."

We haven't said an unkind word since our grandchildren came to live with us. The twin's mother was a kind person and we honor her memory by continuing her kindness. Of course, I think we were kind people to begin with and always try to practice kindness. Don't ask me to prove it, but I think the twins see us as kind people, at least I hope so.

Mark Twain once said, "Kindness is the language which the deaf can hear and the blind can see." Your grandchildren will notice kindness. The wonderful thing about kindness is that it comes back to you. Praise your grandchildren for the kindness they show to family members, pets and friends. You might say, "You're a kind person." Instead of using the word kindness, you may say "You're a good friend to _____," a sentence that implies kindness.

As grandchildren feel more at ease they will start to share stories about friends who haven't been kind. Listen attentively to their stories. After they have finished talking you may sympathize with them and say something like, "I bet that was hard for you." Whatever you say, don't criticize your grandchildren's friends because friendships ebb and flow. Letting your grandchildren work things out for themselves will help them in years to come.

PHRASING AND REPHRASING

Phrasing a sentence involves word choices, pitch, facial expressions, body language, and delivery style. You do these things consciously or unconsciously. As to be expected, when the twins moved in with us they were stressed and short-tempered. My granddaughter said something to her brother in a sharp voice, a bit too sharp for me. Since she was an honors English student I asked her to rephrase her sentence. She grinned at me and restated the sentence in different words and tone.

Phrasing and kindness are linked. In the business world, employees are careful of their phrasing and delivery. I think grandparents need to do the same. When I ask for the twin's help, I do it with a low pitch, action words, and kind words. I keep my sentences short, such as "Would you put this in the attic for me?"

I have to give my grandchildren credit for their word choices and phrasing. They have never spoken to me harshly or started an argument. But your grandchildren, especially infants and toddlers, may have screaming fits and award-winning tantrums. Screaming and tantrums require lots of energy and children usually calm down after a while.

LISTENING FOR SIGNAL WORDS

Sleeping under the bridge was such fun my grandson and his buddies decided to do it again. He sprung the idea on us at the last minute. "We're supposed to have a hard freeze tonight," I countered. "I don't think sleeping under the bridge tonight is a good idea."

"Well, we probably won't do it," he replied. A short while later he said he was going to hang with his friends. At 11:45 p.m. the phone rang. It was a police officer. "I'm here with another officer under the Zumbro River Bridge," he began. "Does the name _____ _____ mean anything to you?"

"That's my grandson," I answered, "and I asked him not to sleep under the bridge tonight."

"Well, we'll talk to the boys," the officer concluded, and hung up.

After this incident I listened for the word "probably" in conversation. Probably could mean yes, or no, or indecision. Later my grandson said the police offers were "really cool" and asked him which high school he attended and which courses he was taking. I don't think he realized the officers were checking his eyes and speech to see if he had been using alcohol or drugs.

When I'm talking with the twins I also listen for the word "hang." This word can mean going to the mall with friends, going to an amusement park, eating together, a sleepover at a friend's house, going to a bonfire, and goodness knows what else. Like "cool," the word "hang" means many things. I ask for more details because "hang" might mean friends are coming over for dinner.

Chances are your grandchildren have signal words, too, and you need to listen for them. A young child might start talking about his or her "blankie," a word that can signal insecurity. A nursery school child may not go anywhere without his or stuffed animal and refer to the animal often in conversation. Being aware of signal words helps us to help our grandchildren. Keep in mind that slang is changing all the time.

RESPONDING TO WORRISOME IDEAS

Our grandson walked in the back door one day and said he and his buddies were going to build a two-level raft. They were going to float down the Zumbro River and stop at a boat landing before the river joined the Mississippi. It was a Huckleberry Finn idea and, though "boys will be boys," we had some concerns. Were the boys good carpenters? Would a two-level raft tip over? How high was the river and would they encounter rapids? Where were they planning to launch the raft?

My husband monitored the boy's progress every step of the way. We were encouraged when we learned our grandson and his friends had an unlimited supply of plastic barrels from a local dairy. These barrels would keep the raft afloat. Since the boys had built a raft last summer, they had some carpentry skills. A kind couple let the boys build the raft in their garage and the construction took several weeks. It was solidly built and even had a slide on the top level. The raft was constructed in two sections so it could be transported to the launch area. The mother of one of the boys was so impressed with the project she called the newspaper.

The newspaper sent a reporter and photographer to the launching. The raft story appeared on the front page of the newspaper next to a story about murder. The contrast between the two stories couldn't have been greater. In the accompanying photo my grandson is standing on the top level and looking into the water.

How do you respond to worrisome ideas? Start with the facts and keep checking them.

Consider your grandchild's experience and skills. Ask yourself, "What's best for my grandchild?" We made encouraging comments, praised our grandson, and praised his friends for their hard work. The raft project became an annual summer event. More important, it created a bond between my grandson and his friends. These guys will probably be at his wedding.

ACTIVE LISTENING, VITAL TO COMMUNICATION

Listening is more than hearing, according to *People Skills* author Robert Bolton, PhD. He defines listening as a combination of "hearing what the other person says and a suspenseful waiting, an intense psychological involvement with the other." You've probably had conversations with people who looked like they were listening, but weren't really paying attention.

Real listening includes psychological involvement and reflective listening skills, according to Bolton. These skills mirror the speaker, involve paraphrasing, talking about feelings, and listening for feeling words. Bolton thinks we have to listen for these words and says, "The reflection of meaning is usually best when it is honed to a single succinct sentence."

Be brief when you reply to your grandchildren. Get to the point, get to it quickly, and keep listening for feeling words. What are some examples of them?

- Funny
- Nervous
- Sad
- Cool
- Sweet
- Ditzy
- Like
- Friend
- Mean
- Nice
- Disorganized
- Organized
- Supportive
- Rely
- Dorky

These are just a few examples. Our grandchildren use feeling words all the time and we are aware of them. Jim Fay and Foster W. Cline, MD, authors of **Grandparenting with Love and Logic,** think listening creates a bond between grandparents and their grandchildren. "Work as hard as you can to do more than just hear your grandchild's words, but to understand what the child means and the importance of these words to him or her," they advise.

Sometimes listening is overhearing. I heard my grandson talking to his sister about the birthday gifts he bought for his girlfriend. The gifts sounded too practical to me. "A bouquet of flowers is always welcome," I commented.

"I also bought her something else," he answered, and described the gift.

"Well, I was just being grandmotherly," I replied.

"I appreciate that," my grandson said. He sounded like he meant it.

HOW TO FRAME THREE-PART ASSERTIONS

Sooner or later, the time comes when you have to be assertive. This can be a challenge because you don't want to hurt your grandchildren or start an argument. Assertions help you to keep grandchildren safe and change behavior. In order to be effective, assertions need to be repeated time and again, something advertisers know all too well. According to Robert Bolton, PhD, an assertion has three parts and you add them together:

Behavior + Feelings + Effects = Assertion

He gives an example of a three-part assertion: "When you don't clean the counter after making snacks, I feel annoyed because it makes more work for me." This assertion works because it has all three parts and it's short. If you're having trouble with assertive statements you may wish to diagram the parts. Practicing your assertions aloud may also help. Here are some of my assertions:

- When you don't finish your laundry I can't do mine and this puts me behind.
- When I got into my car today I was upset to see the gas tank was almost empty and I had to get gas before running errands.
- When you park your car on the street too long I worry about it getting towed away and having to pay a hefty fine.

My examples may not be the boost you need. If you feel insecure about making assertions, write some down and practice them aloud. Listen to the sound of your voice and the words you emphasize. Strive for a matter of fact tone. Your grandchildren may want to practice their assertions as well.

THE ART OF A GENTLE REMINDER

As grandchildren mature and grow, you will have to remind them about homework, appointments, football practice, Scout meetings, and a myriad of other things. Older children may use a white board to remember things. Younger children will enjoy having their own calendars and stickers. Middle school and high school students may want to use personal calendar books with sections for each day of the week.

These reminders should coordinate with the family calendar. Our master calendar hangs on a small bulletin board inside a cupboard door.

While written reminders work well, I think verbal reminders are the best. Reminding your grandchildren of events helps them to figure out lead time and whether your involvement is needed. You may have to drive kids to a sports competition, for example, or band members to an extra practice. I gave my grandchildren advance notice about out-of-town conferences and my writing deadlines.

Keep your reminders short, keep your voice calm, and keep your words to a minimum. You don't want your grandchildren to think you're nagging them. In fact, you might even want to say, "This is my last reminder." Even with reminders, grandchildren may forget things, such as submitting homework on time. If this happens, they are the ones who should pay the consequences, not you. You've already done your homework.

WHAT WORKS

- Monitor your voice pitch and tone.
- Be brief.
- Give sincere compliments.
- Respect children's privacy.
- Be kind in words and deeds.
- Get the facts before you get upset.
- Make a list of signal words and listen for them.
- Practice three-part assertions out loud.

5

GOING "BACK" TO SCHOOL

After their father died, as they had done before, the twins decided when they would return to school. We took turns driving them. My husband had the morning shift and I had the afternoon shift. "The school parking lot is crazy," my grandson said, "so pick us up at the gas station across the road." A footbridge connected the high school with a sidewalk by the gas station and quick stop store. I always arrived early, watched other cars pull up and park, and watched for the twins.

Dozens of students walked across the bridge, laughing and fooling around and, in the winter time, sliding in the snow. But my grandson and granddaughter were far from exuberant. They walked slowly, rarely interacted with other students, and looked like grieving, despondent teenagers. I understood this, for I was their grieving, despondent grandmother. Their mom should be picking up the twins from school, not me, and I held back my tears.

To keep my mind occupied I tried to read the newspaper. The mental trick didn't work and there were days when I did cry. Yet I tried to greet the twins cheerfully and start a conversation on the way home. Occasionally the twins would make a comment, but they were usually silent and the silence was deafening.

Looking back now, I think they were worried about how they would fit in with us and worried about the future. Reversing roles, I thought about how I would feel if both of my parents had died. I would be worried, too, even a little bit frightened of my grandparents. Just like the twins, I would keep a low profile, hunker down, and see what developed. Several months later the twins received their driver's licenses and drove to school in their mother's green van. We were glad and so were they.

In recent years many schools have become aware of grandparents. When the twins were in elementary school and living in another community, they invited us to Grandparents Day. My husband was working at the time and couldn't go, so I went, and the hour and half drive was worth it. As I walked toward the school entrance I saw a chalk message on the side-walk, "Welcome Harriet Hodgson, Author!" As I neared the entrance I saw the same chalk message again. And again.

The messages were written by my granddaughter and they touched my heart. She knew I was an author and wanted to acknowledge the fact.

Before moving the family to Rochester our daughter, a composite engineer with an MBA degree and six industry certifications, lived in several different towns. Though distance separated us, we stayed in touch, and attended as many school functions as we could, including concerts and science fairs. While our involvement in the twin's education continued in high school, it was a different kind of involvement.

WAYS TO PARTICIPATE AT SCHOOL

Many school systems are trying to involve grandparents in activities. Dr. Salman Al-Azami and Ian Gyllenspetz cite some of these activities in their booklet, "Grandparents and Grandchildren: Learning Together," published by The Basic Skills Agency in London, England. Schools can tap grandparents' talents, such as playing a musical instrument, teaching computers sills, story-telling, sharing life stories, helping with sports, staffing fair booths, and more. Involving grandparents benefits both generations, younger and older, and also impacts the community.

Children benefit because of the bond created between grandparents and grandchildren. Schools benefit by expanding the knowledge base. "All schools that have involved grandparents have reported improved standards in English and mathematics," they authors write. Being involved at school is reassuring to grandparents like you and me and makes us feel valued.

Participation in school activities is voluntary. Working grandparents may not have the time to volunteer at school. After losing four family members in nine months, my husband and I were so overwhelmed we couldn't volunteer for anything. However, we could contribute by attending meetings, such as the gymnastic team's mandatory session about drug addiction, donating money, and going to school events.

We loved the choir concerts, band concerts, and plays. One of our granddaughter's friends was in a musical. "Would you like to go," she asked tentatively. "I'd be glad to get the tickets."

"Sure, we'd love to go," I answered, and we enjoyed the musical thoroughly. Going to the musical was a way to show support for our granddaughter's friends and school activities. Your grandchildren's school may not have much connection with grandparents. If you have time, contact the school and offer to help. Some things you could do:

- Read to young children.
- Provide one-to-one tutoring in math.
- Be a lunch room helper and monitor.
- Plant a vegetable garden with student help and maintain it.
- Share your talents: playing the piano, violin, scrabble, drawing, etc. (I've spoken to elementary children about writing.)
- Give a talk about your occupation or native country.
- Work at school fairs and sports events.
- Translate school notices and newsletters into another language.
- Collect donated books for the school library.
- Straighten messy storerooms.
- Donate food to a bake sale.

You will probably think of other ways to help at school. I recently read a blog posting by a grandmother who took homemade cookies to her grandson's class. Her grandson was uncomfortable with her gesture and she was not. She felt her gesture made a statement to the teacher and the school: I'm here to help. I applaud this proactive grandma.

PARTICIPATION BARRIERS

GRGs and GAPs face many participation barriers. Grieving for multiple losses was our barrier and it wasn't one we could surmount easily. Overcoming the barrier took us years. We were so affected by multiple losses we could hardly think. To be honest, I remember little about 2007 and, in order to refresh my memory, I read the book and journal I wrote that year. If I hadn't written these books, my memory would be nil.

I have fragmented memories, however, and during a recent conversation with my grandson referred to something that happened. "I don't remember it," he admitted. "I don't remember much about that year."

"I hardly remember it myself," I replied.

For many grandparents language is a barrier, a brick wall that keeps them from understanding school events or participating in them. A report, "Involving Immigrant and Refugee Families in Their Children's Schools: Barriers, Challenges and Successful Strategies," funded by a US Department of Education grant, details some of these barriers. The lack of bilingual staff in schools is one barrier. School materials printed in English only is another.

You may also face a cultural barrier. Where you come from, schools may act independently and families may not get involved. Rather, schools and teachers are trusted to do their jobs. "Language minority parents [and grandparents] may come from cultures where parents are not expected to take an active role in their children's educational experiences," the report notes.

Isolation is another barrier and may be due to your health problems, failing health, violent neighborhood, or lack of transportation, including public transportation.

Many grandparents, and you may be one, continue to work in order to put food on the table for their grandchildren. Work hours prevent you from participating in school activities. At the end of the day, you're so tired you wonder if you'll be able to fix a meal, yet manage to do it.

I had a work problem and still have it. Because I'm a freelancer I work at home. Many people don't know I'm working, or don't take my work seriously, so I'm constantly interrupted by phone calls. Thank goodness emails can wait until I have time to get to them. While I'm writing I'm doing laundry, keeping up with the book business, starting dinner, and other tasks. At three in the afternoon I take a coffee or tea break and watch television.

"You must think I spend the day on the couch," I commented to my granddaughter. She looked at me and smiled.

"Grandma, I've been living with you for years and I know how hard you work." Her reply made me want to shout "Hallelujah!"

OUT-OF-POCKET EDUCATION COSTS

Financial problems are a huge barrier and, across this nation, many grandparents struggle to pay school expenses. Glenda Phillips Reynolds and her colleges discuss financial issues in their article, "The Roles of Grandparents in Educating Today's Children." The grandparents who are raising their grandchildren may spend down their savings to care for the next generation. As the authors write, "Grandparents sometimes feel disappointment mixed with anger, guilt and concern about finances . . . The children may feel abandoned even if they are grateful to grandparents."

Education has changed vastly since you and I were in school. When I was in high school notebook paper was provided, if you can believe it, and there were no fees for participating in sports. Today, children have to bring their own supplies to school, pay to participate in sports (the fees keep going up) and sell products to pay for sports programs. Like all of the gymnasts on the team, my granddaughter sold buttery coffee cakes to help cover expenses. We had coffee cakes in the freezer for months.

Personally, I don't think we're helping students when we force them to become hucksters. So many students that come to the door are embarrassed. Others look dejected when we tell them we have pounds and pounds of popcorn leftover from last year. While my husband and I try to help, we can't buy something from every student that is raising funds.

The cost of school supplies adds up quickly and some grandparents can't pay them. Greensboro, North Carolina, conducts a school donation drive for grandparents who are raising their grandchildren. Donated supplies, backpacks full of stuff, are dropped off at the Greensboro Senior Center or other centers. Your community may not have a donation program like this, but a local business, radio station, or television may conduct one. Watch the newspaper and television for announcements.

THE SITTER ISSUE

It's guaranteed. The day will come when you need a sitter. Sitters can help children to become independent and self-confident. But your situation is different. Your grandchildren may already feel insecure and the thought of a sitter adds to their insecurity. Indeed, your grandchildren may feel abandoned and alone. How you help them?

- Arrange for the sitter to visit beforehand.
- Give the sitter a list of your house rules.
- Tell your grandchildren where you're going and when you will return. If your grandchildren can't read yet, draw a picture of a clock with the hands set at your return time.
- Plan activities for when you're gone. Make sure you have the necessary materials for these activities.
- Give your grandchildren something to look forward to after you return, such as making popcorn and watching a movie.

Provide a list for the sitter with contact information for your destination and emergency phone numbers. There are many free sitter checklists on the Internet. Today, many sitters ask friends over to sit with them though the friends aren't paid. Before you contact the sitter, think about your stand on this issue.

Since our grandchildren were teenagers they didn't need sitters. After a year as GRGs my husband and I felt we needed a break and decided to attend a medical meeting in Los Angeles. While we had no concerns about our grandchildren, we were concerned about other teens at school. Our concerns came from real-life stories. Two of my husband's colleagues left town for a week and when they returned they were shocked to find their houses had been trashed. Another came home and found his new car was instantly old and ready for the junk yard. We didn't want to happen to our family.

"Don't you trust us?" my granddaughter asked.

"We trust you, but we're worried about other kids at school," my husband answered. "You won't say we're gone, yet the word could still get out." We arranged for our granddaughter to stay with a friend and our grandson to stay with the man our daughter had planned to marry. They were fine with these plans, had a good week at school, and we had the break we needed.

FINDING THE BEST NURSERY SCHOOL

I taught nursery school for six years and loved every one. Nursery school kids have good vocabularies and observation skills, yet the world can be a confusing place. "I bet you have a bed at school," one of my students said. His idea was so surprising I arranged for my morning and afternoon classes to visit my home. Afterwards a boy told his mother, "Teacher's house is cleaner than ours." I wonder how that went over!

How do you find the best nursery school? Answer these questions before you enroll your grandchild.

- Is the school accredited by the state?
- Are the teachers certified?
- What is the teacher-student ratio? In the state of Minnesota, for example, nursery schools are required to have one teacher for every 10 children.
- Is there enough square footage for the number of enrolled students?
- Do children have free access to art materials, books, games, toys?
- Does the school schedule times for physical activity?
- Are the snacks healthy?
- Are there enough bathrooms and are they clean?
- What is the school's safety policy?

- Can parents and grandparents visit at any time?
- Does the school have a good reputation?

I think you should also learn about the school's basic philosophy. The school I taught at was founded by a Mayo Clinic physician and local educators. Its philosophy of putting children first was, and continues to be, evident in the school curriculum. Staff turnover is another thing to check out. Whether it's at a nursery school, grade school, or high school, a high turnover is cause for concern. You should really be concerned if teachers are leaving in clusters.

TRANSPORTATION ISSUES

Transportation can be a problem for parents and grandparents alike. Several taxi services in my town transport children to and from school. If your home is in a different part of town your grandchildren may not be eligible for bus service. Our daughter bought her house because she wanted the twins to go to a specific school. Then the school district moved the boundary. Neighbors gathered together and paid for a school bus themselves, something the district permitted.

When the twins moved in with us they were no longer eligible for bus transportation. I talked to the principal and he checked into the problem. A transportation person called us. "We've found service for your grandchildren," she began, "but they will be on the bus for more than an hour before they get to school." Our grandchildren were already on an early schedule and bus transportation would make it even earlier, so we drove the twins to school for several months.

While calling the school district yields information, for best results, I would go to the administration offices and plead your case in person. Get as much specific information as you can, including location of the bus stop, pick-up time, and any additional fees you may have to pay.

HELPING WITH HOMEWORK

Raising your grandchildren means you're involved in homework. Michele Borba, EdD, examines the homework issue in a Parenting Bookmark website article, "Hot Homework Tips for Parents." She says adults need to realize they are helpers and not doers. "Sometimes in our quest to help our kids succeed, we may get carried away by providing too much help," she explains. Borba thinks effort, and not just the end product, should be praised. Doing their homework helps grandchildren learn the values of hard work and perseverance.

Helping with homework gives us a chance to get to know our grandchildren better. My grandchildren asked me to proofread some English papers. While I agreed to this request, I also told them I was looking for errors only, not trying to change their style. One of my grandson's papers was so intellectual I had to read it several times. Finally, I realized he had lost some words in the text editing process. "This paragraph doesn't make sense," I said cautiously. My grandson read the paragraph and agreed with me.

Some grandchildren like to do their homework right after school. Others like to take a break and do their homework after supper. Homework is easier when children do it at the same time each day and in the same place. Our grandchildren have their own desks, but not their own printers. We have an in-house computer network and the printer is in the lower-level office. While I'm writing I've often been startled by the printer belching out prose.

The US Government includes practical ideas in a website article, "Homework Tips for Parents." These tips apply to GRGs and GAPs as well. The publication divides homework into three categories, practice, preparation and extension. "Parent [or grandparent] can confuse children if the teaching techniques they use differ from those in the classroom," the article cautions. Thank goodness the twins never asked me to help with math homework because I couldn't do it.

You can help your grandchildren with homework by having a positive attitude, keeping materials on hand, and providing guidance, not answers, the article notes. "If homework is meant to be done by your child alone, stay away." Grandchildren may be willing to do their homework but have difficulty fitting it into a day. This is where we come in, and we can make sure our grandchildren have a nutritious snack or meal before doing their homework and a quiet and comfortable place to work.

If learning is difficult for your grandchild you may wish to get a tutor. A retired teacher may be willing to coach your grandchild. You may wish to arrange for vision and hearing checks. If you think reading is the cause of the problem, have your grandchild evaluated by a reading specialist or dyslexia tutor.

Thinking about homework made me recall a desk in our deceased daughter's living room. The desk was really a dressing table that belonged to my mother. Our daughter stripped off the old varnish and painted the desk white. When we were clearing out their house we asked the twins for permission to donate the desk to Goodwill. They agreed. A few days later, one of our granddaughter's friends mentioned the used desk she had just purchased for her college dorm room. She loved the desk and we loved the story. My mother's desk had found a new home.

AFTERSCHOOL ACTIVITIES

Afterschool activities have many benefits. Your grandchildren get to be with friends, make new friends, and learn new skills in a safe environment. Girl Scouts and gymnastics were my granddaughter's afterschool activities. My grandson was involved in the Scrabble Club and Boy Scouts for a while. Both of them were inducted into the National Honor Society and were involved in service projects. For his service, my grandson worked on Habitat for Humanity houses and donated blood. My granddaughter made blankets for a community organization and volunteered for school events.

Afterschool activities are available when classes are over. "Children and youth who attend afterschool programs do better in school, and are safer and less likely to get into trouble in the hours after the end of a school day," according to an Internet article. The article, "Why are Afterschool Programs Good for School-Age Children and Youth?" is on the Concept to Classroom website. Benefits of afterschool programs are cited in the article and they include better reading skills, improved school attendance, submitting better quality homework, and high aspirations for the future.

Some school systems hire teachers specifically for these add-on programs. Other school systems may rely on volunteers.

The National AfterSchool Association has established a code of ethics for activities outside the regular school day. Safety comes first and the code states that no harm will come to any child. The code also states the responsibilities of afterschool professionals. You may still be feeling your way as a GRG or GAP and afterschool activities aren't on your To Do list now. Still, you need to know what is available. The school office should be able to provide you with this information.

PARENT CONFERENCES: SHOULD YOU GO?

Walking into school for your first parent conference may bring back memories of your children's early years. Parent-teacher conferences are a way to assess a grandchild's progress and, even more important, make plans to work together. Because I'm a former teacher, I'm all for parent conferences and so is my husband. We never went to one. The first year the twins lived with us we missed parent conferences because we were overcome with grief and daily life.

My husband and I felt bad about this and promised ourselves we would go next time. But we missed conferences again because we heard about them too late. "When are parent conferences?" I asked.

"Oh, they were last week," my grandson replied.

"We never heard anything about them," I countered.

My granddaughter joined the conversation. "Conferences are for parents of kids who are having trouble and getting bad grades," she explained. "We're not."

Clearly, our grandchildren didn't want us to attend parent conferences and we respected their wishes. Parent night was a crowded night, the twins said, and you had to wait in long lines to speak to the teachers. I think the twins didn't want us to attend parent conferences because we weren't their parents. It's that simple and I understand it. Just as the twins said, they were doing well, and both of them had A averages.

Busy as your days are, I hope you find the time to go to parent conferences. When parents and teachers work together children do better. You will be an informed grandparent, which is another plus. Attending your first parent conference can be the beginning of a year-long partnership that benefits your grandchildren.

SCHOOL TRIPS AND TRAVEL

The twin's high school planned a science trip to Chicago and both of them wanted to go. We were all for it. Chicago is an exciting city and the trip sounded like it was planned well. It was a successful trip and the twins talked about it for several days. My grandson also took a trip to Orlando, Florida, with the high school marching band. "We marched down the main street of Disney World and everyone was applauding," he recalled. "It was really hot and we were wearing wool uniforms, but it was still fun."

He also went to Spain with a group from his Spanish class. Thirty students originally signed up for the trip, but as the economy sagged, many took their names off the list. When we took our grandson to the school parking lot, the departure point for the trip, there were only six people and one of them was the father of a student. Everyone was excited, talking in animated voices, and eager to leave. They landed in Madrid, went to Toledo, Grenada and Majorca. "The food was amazing," my grandson said. "Paella, chorizo, octopus.

"I split a fried octopus sandwich with my teacher and it was the best sandwich I ever ate."

Three weeks later we picked up our grandson at the Minneapolis-St. Paul airport. He was one of the last ones off the plane and he was grinning from ear to ear. When our grandson went to get his luggage off the carousel the Spanish teacher approached us. "Your grandson is a fine young man, and I wanted you to know that," she said.

Our granddaughter went on her international trip at the end of her senior year. The tour started in Dublin, Ireland, continued in Wales, Liverpool, Edinburgh Scotland, and London. "Edinburgh was my favorite place and we stayed there for three days. I would love to go there again," she said. International trips bring textbook information to life and foster understanding. Better yet, they give students a chance to speak a different language and try new foods. Our granddaughter is a talented photographer and her photographs of the trip are stunning. In case you're wondering, we bought trip insurance for the twins. Each of them had Euro currency and tip money for the bus drivers and tour guides.

RELIGIOUS EDUCATION

Our granddaughter continued to attend the church her mother had joined. We invited our grandson to our church, but he wasn't interested in going. The twins were being pushed and pulled in various directions and we didn't want to pressure them about religious education. Besides, we believe religious education is more than services, classes, and meetings; it is how you practice your faith at home, in the community and the world.

I think the twins learned about our religious beliefs by watching us in action. They are very aware of how respect-fully we treat each other and our volunteer efforts in the community.

You may belong to a religious community that has a youth minister, priest or rabbi. Take advantage of this person and seek his or her help. What suggestions does this person have? Are there helpful books in the church or synagogue library? Is there a forthcoming event for kids, such as a sleepover? When all is said and done, talk with your grandchildren and see how they want to approach religious education. Attending Sunday school or services with a friend may be an option.

Faith can help grandchildren find their way through dark and confusing times. But as Bob Deits wisely points out *Life After Loss*, religious faith can't immunize children against loss, bring back the deceased, or serve as a grief recovery shortcut. However, faith can be a source of comfort. "You will be able to accept new places, new stages of life," Deits writes. Faith can help grandchildren feel less alone and see hope ahead.

COLLEGE/UNIVERSITY WEEKENDS FOR PARENTS

Today, many colleges and universities host special week-ends for parents. Usually these weekends are held in the fall. The twins didn't say much about the parent weekends at their colleges. We didn't know whether to go or stay home and fi-nally asked, "Do you want us to come?" Both said they weren't interested in parents' weekend. We respected their wishes. I think they didn't want us to come for the same reasons they didn't want us to go to parent conferences.

You may be wondering if you should attend parents' weekend at your grandchild's college or university. The only suggestion I have is to talk with your grandchild. Assure him or her that you will respect their opinion. Mail a box of goodies to your grandchild and send it in time for the weekend. In my experience, grandchildren always appreciate a box from home. Though we're not physically at parents' weekend, we are there in spirit.

WHAT WORKS

- Find ways to participate at school.
- Track out-of-pocket school expenses.
- Help with homework but don't provide answers.
- Encourage your grandchildren to participate in after-school activities.
- Attend parent conferences if you feel comfortable doing it.
- Respect grandchildren's wishes.

6

STRESS THAT KEEPS YOU AWAKE AT NIGHT

As the years passed I settled into the GRG groove. I knew what I was supposed to be doing and kept at it, but wondered if I was doing it well. Was I giving my grandchildren the support they needed? Often I awakened from a sound sleep, thinking about the twins and the rating they might give me. Hopefully, I would get at least three stars for trying.

Authors Jim Fay and Foster W. Cline, MD, in their book *Grandparenting with Love & Logic*, say grandparenting is pretty straightforward. "It is the interaction people have with their grandchildren," they explain. "Played out in life, however, grandparenting comes in a variety of forms." Being a GRG or GAP comes in a variety of forms as well. You may have a different grandparenting style than I have or your style may be similar.

All grandparents who are raising their grandchildren are stressed. Time may be a stressor and, no matter how hard you try, you never get everything done. Money may be a stressor and you can't make ends meet. In fact, with skyrocketing grocery, gas, and clothing prices you are falling behind. Your biggest stressor is seeing grandchildren in pain. Their pain is your pain and it is terrible.

PAIN OF SEEING GRANDCHILDREN IN PAIN

Diane Berman writes about pain in her article, "Supporting Your Teenager Through Grief and Loss." Even if your grandchildren haven't lost their parents as mine have, a major life upheaval such as moving may be a source of pain. "As a parent [or grandparent] we want to be able to take a child's pain away," Berman notes. Time and again, I've wished I could feel my grandchildren's pain for them.

I've had a challenging life and know the only way to get rid of pain is to accept it. In my experience, accepting pain shortens its duration. Now that I'm a grandmother, I realize life's tragedies have made me stronger. Becoming a GRG has made me stronger as well. The most important thing I've learned is that I'm a survivor. Grandchildren also learn from emotional pain and, as they grow older, develop coping skills and self-worth.

Children have to learn how to handle pain for themselves. Learning how to cope is a basic skill. An article on the LiveStrong website, "List of Life Skills Children Should Have," says skills include financial management, teamwork, etiquette and managing emotions. "Kids must learn how to manage their emotions, especially in stressful or upsetting situations," the article notes.

Learning to manage emotions takes practice. Like adults, sometimes children manage their emotions well and other times they "lose it." You can help grandchildren by reading stories to them, providing art materials, linking them to nature and your religious/spiritual community. Older children may wish to keep a journal or diary. Another option is to write a book about their experiences. Very young children are capable of telling and illustrating stories.

When I was teaching nursery school I had my students draw "angry pictures." I put out white drawing paper and a variety of colored markers. The kids chatted about what made them angry as they were drawing, things like a sibling breaking a toy. Red and black seemed to be the dominant colors and many drawings were toothy. One boy drew a picture of himself snarling. His oversized, fang-like teeth dominated the drawing and were so threatening I expected them to jump off the paper and bite me.

How do grandchildren learn to cope with pain? They learn by watching you. Whether you like it or not, you're their role model. Your grandkids are gathering data constantly, your traits, values, coping skills, evaluation skills, problem-solving, respect for others, and trustworthiness. Bit by bit, these observations teach them how to cope. Years from now, they will remember your example.

So here's the truth of the grandparenting story. You can't keep grandkids from pain. You can't feel pain for them. You can't inoculate them against pain. You can't put on a show to entertain them. You can't guarantee their happiness. But you can let them grow and mature and learn for themselves. Even better, you can do what grandparents do best, love them, and keep assuring them of your love.

PEERS AND PEER SUPPORT

Peers affect your grandchildren's thinking. Clothing trends are a good example. Students at the twin's high school began wearing pajama bottoms instead of jeans. When I saw a crowd of kids coming out the main door I thought to myself, "Hmmm. Those kids look like they're wearing pajamas." They were.

My granddaughter wore plaid pajama bottoms to school and I didn't say a word. Sometimes silence is the better approach.

Clothing trends come and go quickly and so may peers. A peer group is a group of friends about the same age. Members of the group stay in constant touch with each other. Over time, the members forge a strong bond. Close as they seem, some members will drift away when the going gets tough. The twins belonged to separate peer groups and I could hardly keep track of all of their friends. "I need photo IDs!" I exclaimed.

Peer groups may divide into sub-groups. My grandson's group divided into a sub-group of about five and they went fishing and camping together. My granddaughter's group divided into a sub-group of three. They went to movies, baked cookies at our house, stayed overnight, and visited Ireland, Scotland and England together. At first, I was concerned about a group of three because one person might feel left out. But the threesome continued and I thought of them as female musketeers, all for onc and one for all. These friends remain close.

One evening my daughter returned from watching a movie with a friend. "You're supposed to feel good after seeing a chick flick," she said. "After this one we felt terrible."

I understood her feelings completely. "Oh, I bought the book and tried to read it, but it was so terrible I threw it out," I replied.

"It's awful," she said. "A real downer."

"It's awful," I agreed.

I enjoyed this conversation because we were communicating on the same level, something that can be rare in a grandparent-grandchild relationship.

The twin's peer groups helped them immensely. Friends stayed with them through thick and thin, as the saying goes.

My granddaughter remains in contact with her friends via Skype. My grandson stays in contact with friends via text messaging. Without the support of peers, I don't think the twins would be doing as well as they are today. When I see their friends I want to hug them and thank them, but I don't because they would be embarrassed.

Be thankful for your grandchildren's friends. Some may even become lifelong friends. So what if they make lots of noise. So what if they mess up the kitchen. So what if they stay up until the wee hours of the morning. So what if they take your favorite spot on the couch. Your grandchildren have supportive friends and that's a blessing.

BUDGETING AND HOUSING WOES

Our grocery bills increased fourfold after the twins moved in with us. I thought the bills would double, not quadruple, and am still astonished at how much we spend on food when the twins are home. To keep pace with their appetites I go to the store every other day, and keep the refrigerator packed with food. Still, the twins open the door and peer inside with the intensity of spelunkers assessing a new cave. "Is there anything for lunch?" they ask.

Anything for lunch? I just spent $130 on groceries. Though we kept accurate tax records for the court, we didn't keep records about food, power, or gas bills. Our electric bills shot up because of three computers in the house, extra showers, and additional laundry.

According to a Cornell University website article, GRGs and GAPs face many financial challenges. "The costs of raising a child(ren) is likely to impact your budget or retirement fund," the article notes. From personal experience, I can tell you it takes weeks to average your costs and budget for them. The twins received Social Security checks and we spent the money as directed, on their education (field trips, international trips) and a car for school transportation.

Your grandchildren may be eligible for scholarships. The nursery school I taught at had tuition scholarships for children. Contact the school principal and ask to meet with him or her about scholarship availability and requirements. Community organizations, such as Rotary, may also offer scholarships.

Coming up with the cash for food, clothing and shelter is hard enough, but you may not have enough room for grandchildren. You feel like you're living in a tuna fish can. Worse, you may be paying rent for substandard or severely substandard housing. An income-based apartment may be the solution. With income-based housing the Housing and Urban Development Agency (HUD) pays part of your rent. To qualify, you must meet minimum and maximum income restrictions. For more information on income-based housing contact your local HUD office.

Communities across the country are waking up to grandfamily housing needs. Phoenix, Arizona, for example, built two apartment buildings, with a total of 56 units. Forty-four units have two-bedrooms and 12 units have three bedrooms. Funding for the Grandfamilies Place of Phoenix comes from Low Income Housing Tax Credit and the City of Phoenix Home Investment Partnership Program.

Milwaukee, Wisconsin, has also built apartments for grandfamilies. Tom Daykin describes the project in a "Journal Sentinel" article. The 47-unit Villard Square is the first of its kind in Milwaukee. New York City and Boston have built similar apartments. Do you need lower cost housing? Contact the local Area Council on Aging, senior center, or Department of Social Services. If that doesn't get results, write a letter to the editor of the newspaper.

CONNFLICT BETWEEN PROTECTION AND FREEDOM

Every morning at 4:30 a.m. my daughter tumbled out of bed and dressed for work. Her commuting time was an hour and a half each way. She was in charge of three production lines at an engine manufacturing plant. The twins were used to getting up on their own, having juice and cereal for breakfast, and racing to the bus stop. In the summer time they roamed freely, going on long bike trips, hikes, or hanging out with friends.

Sometimes we took the twins to museums or the family cabin, but otherwise they were independent. When our grandchildren moved in with us we set some boundaries. These boundaries provided structure at an unstructured time in their lives. Boundary number one was keeping us informed of any changes in plans. If they didn't call, we reminded them of this boundary. "But we're not used to this," my grandson complained. Well, we weren't used to it either.

The family had already suffered two car crashes and our biggest fear was a third, especially after the twins had their driver's licenses. Our granddaughter had a few fender benders. Despite the big side mirrors, she couldn't see the back of the van. We were so concerned for the twin's safety we bought another car. After visiting several car dealers we found a car we thought would "fit" our granddaughter.

She got in the driver's seat, adjusted the levers, and realized she could see forward, backward, and sideways. Our grandson was on a field trip that day, so he didn't see the car. However, we called him and told him about it. It is black and has just about every gadget a car can have. As dealers would say, "It's loaded." When our grandson saw the car he inspected all of the extras, especially the sound system. "Cool!" he exclaimed.

The car gave the twins more freedom. We wanted them to have freedom and, at the same time, needed to protect them. There were times when the twins felt constrained by our rules. Still, our mission was to love them, protect them and meet the court's requirements. Certainly, we didn't want to be accused of child endangerment. Years from now, when the twins have their children, they will understand the push-pull of parenting and grandparenting.

The push: Nudging the twins towards adulthood. The pull: Bringing them back to safety. Parents and grandparents need to pick their battles, according to Christina Frank's article, "The Need for Parenting Consistency," posted on the Parenting website. Frank's advice: "Make rules. . . and bend some of them." Our rules were specific to our family situation. Your grandchildren may object to your rules but, if truth be told, they're probably grateful for them. If they don't want to do something they can always say, "My grandparents won't let me."

LITTLE OR NO TIME FOR MARRIAGE MAINTENANCE

Ever since we married 55 years ago we've had a close relationship. Friends often comment on our closeness. Suffering multiple losses in 2007 brought us even closer. Our daughter's death brought us closer still. I'm fortunate to have a husband who shares his feelings and is comfortable doing it. Other grandparents raising grandchildren aren't as fortunate.

On one GRG blog a grandmother criticizes her husband for not helping more. A posting on another website tells how grandparents are working together for the welfare of their grandchildren. We have a team approach to marriage and life. The instant I told our grandchildren they were coming home with us we became a GRG team and our team efforts continue to this day.

We accepted the fact that we wouldn't have much time alone. Our schedules depended then, and partially depend now, on the twin's schedules. Yet every morning we begin the day with hugs. Each of us thanks the other for our life together. Every day we say "I love you." And every day I thank my husband for putting up with my creative personality. Our marriage has survived the year he spent in Vietnam, financial losses and gains, and outside interference. Each year is better than the last and our marriage continues to thrive.

Why is our marriage different? Before we married we went together for four years, so we knew each other well. We planned our lives and followed these plans. Most important, we respect and trust each other.

John M. Grohol, PsyD, writes about strong marriages in his PsyhCentral article, "5 Secrets to a Successful Long-Term Relationship or Marriage." Grohol thinks marriage needs constant attention in order to work. He lists five characteristics of a good marriage. I've changed the wording and added personal comments.

1. **Compromise.** Our marriage began with an important compromise. I would teach and my husband would go to

medical school. My starting salary in a Minneapolis suburb was $4,050 and we kept track of every penny. I made weekly menus and shopped with such care a grocery store employee thought I was a home economics teacher.

2. **Communicate.** Since we had been communicating for four years we continued this communication. Honesty was our approach then and is our approach now. We often talk about our feelings to see if the other feels the same way.

3. **Choose your battles.** This point makes us chuckle because we've never had an argument. Though we may differ on issues, we differ with civility and respect. We have never shouted at one another and never will. Why would I shout at the man I love? Instead of competing, as some couples do, we support one another.

4. **Express your needs.** Early on, I realized a medical student's wife, and later a physician's wife, had to have her own identity. Having my own identity doesn't alter the support I give my husband. I'm my husband's booster and he is mine. "What's your next book going to be about?" he often asks.

5. **Be trustworthy and honest.** Trust and honesty are the foundation of our marriage. Even people who meet us for the first time can see our trust, honesty, and mutual support.

Grohol concludes his article with an important point: "You need to show attention and nurture the relationship constantly, just as you would nurture anything you value in life." Like many who are raising their grandchildren, however, we had to deal with outside interference. In fact, outside interference proved to be our biggest challenge.

OUTSIDE INTERFERENCE

People sympathize with you and want to help. During our grandparenting journey we've heard many "you should" statements. Statements are one thing and actions are another. One family, strangers we didn't know, crossed family boundaries and their interference lasted for months. Maybe they thought we were demented. Certainly, their actions indicated a lack of trust in our abilities and their interference became meddling.

The problem with outside interference is that it comes from people who aren't raising their grandchildren. These well-meaning people are looking from the outside in, and don't have all the facts. What they know, or think they know, can be inaccurate or even false. Finally, they don't know anything about you. Outside interference can harm your grandchild or grandchildren. What can you say to someone who is meddling?

- Thanks for that idea. I'll give it some thought.
- We've already taken care of the problem, but thank you.
- My grandchildren are getting the support and care they need.
- While I appreciate your concern, this conversation is making me uncomfortable.
- You are crossing our family boundaries. Please stop.

Sadly, outside interference may actually be inside interference, trouble with your child, the parent of your grandchild. Millie Ferrer-Chancy and her colleagues address this issue in their article, "Grandparents Raising Grandchildren: Understanding Relationships." You can diffuse the situation by not jumping to conclusions, saying unkind words, or placing blame. Instead, you can be a good listener and try to see things from the other person's viewpoint. "Agree to disagree if you are unable to resolve conflict right away," the article advises.

Encouraging parent visits may also diffuse the situation. However, these visits should be consistent with legal decisions. As much as you hope, as hard as you try, your efforts may be unsuccessful, and you have to let go. Letting go is a painful process, one that happens gradually. You don't have to fix everything, the authors continue. "Remember, your child is an adult and can make her or his own choices as well as experience the consequences of these choices."

If the outside interference doesn't stop you may wish to consult a lawyer. Keeping a Memo for Record (dated narratives and descriptions) is a good idea. Though we didn't keep this memo or talk directly to the parents, we sought professional help, met with our minister and increased our caregiving efforts. The twins settled in, became part of the family, and the outside interference stopped. I think the twins discussed the issue privately and worked out solutions together.

HEALTH INSURANCE

Chances are your health insurance plan, if you have one, won't cover grandchildren's medical costs. We were fortunate. The twin's father, a master electrician, had health coverage through his union. His plan also covered the twins and they carry their insurance cards with them. Thank goodness. In August my grandson and his friends drove to Florida to visit a buddy who had joined the military. While they were playing disc golf, his friend lost a disc and my grandson went to look for it. He accidentally ran into a palm frond and the jagged edge scratched the cornea of his eye.

He called my husband for advice. My husband asked him to describe his symptoms, told him to wait an hour, and said he would call back. During the second call the scratched cornea was confirmed and my husband told him to go to the nearest hospital emergency room, where he received excellent care. By the time he returned home his eye had almost healed. "How many grandchildren can call their Grandpa and get medical advice?" I asked.

"No kidding," my grandson replied. The twins are glad to have a doctor in the house and I am as well.

K. R. Tremblay and others discuss health insurance in their Colorado State University website article, "Grandparents: As Parents." While grandchildren may be covered by a military insurance plan for retirees called CHAMPUS, it may not cover the grandchildren in your care. In order for your grandchildren to be covered you may have to adopt them. But thankfully, "several states passed legislation requiring group health insurance companies to include dependent grandchildren." As you might expect, some companies are fighting this legislation.

For more information on health coverage contact your state Department of Legal Services. The American Bar Association Center for Children and Law can also provide some answers.

Medicaid is also an option. The Medicaid plan is for families or individuals with low incomes, according to a University of Florida website article by Maisie Ross and colleagues. This insurance covers medical, mental health, and dental care. Florida also has a Child Health Check-Up

Program. Grandchildren who qualify for Medicaid coverage also qualify for this program.

GRANDCHILDREN'S MEDICAL AND DENTAL BILLS

Growing children need medical/dental care. My grandson had his wisdom teeth removed and the procedure was covered by his father's insurance plan. This plan will continue to cover the twin's medical bills as long as they are students. Many colleges and universities offer student medical and dental plans. The University of Minnesota, for example, requires all full-time students to have health insurance and, according to its website, "places significant restrictions on the type of insurance that may be used." Students may also get private health insurance or enroll in a group plan. Your local Department of Public Health Services should be able to give you insurance advice and leads. There may be a free dental clinic in your town.

PERSONAL HEALTH PROBLEMS

Considering my age, it's not surprising that I have some health problems and high blood pressure is one of them. I take prescribed medicine to slow my heart rate. The medicine also causes cramps in my calf muscles. For these reasons, I stopped and rested on a stairway landing in the public library. A library executive, someone I know, walked up the stairway and saw me. "I take blood pressure medicine and had to rest," I explained.

"That's okay. The research department isn't going anywhere," he answered kindly.

My husband also takes medicine for high blood pressure, so we're quite a pair. The medication altered our walking program. Instead of walking briskly as we used to, we walk slowly. Though we're capable of walking miles, we're less apt to do it because our legs might cramp. Both of us are also salt sensitive and have to watch our daily consumption.

We are also hard of hearing and wear hearing aids. Even with hearing aids we may not understand sentences, especially if the television is on or if one of us is in another room. The twins are used to this and often repeat sentences for us. When we go to Rotary meetings we may not hear everything the speaker says and rely on lip reading.

While cooking for teenagers is fun, I've gained some weight, and have to lose about 15 pounds. Dropping the weight is hard because I can't walk as far. Still, I'm determined to do it. We're eating smaller servings and I'm preparing meals with no salt and little fat. You won't see a salt shaker on our table. The best person to take care of my health is me and I'm not giving up on myself.

Have you neglected your health lately? In his book, **Straight Talk About Death for Teenagers**, Earl A. Grollman makes a wise statement: "Neglecting your health won't bring your loved one back to life." His point could be expanded to "Neglecting your health won't make your grandchildren's parent(s) any better." Each day, as you wake up, I hope you will make a promise to yourself: "I will take care of me so I can take care of my grandchildren."

FEELING OF LOSS

Asleep or awake, a feeling of loss lingers in the back of your mind. That is understandable. You are raising your grandchildren because of a loss. As Rabbi Grollman noted in one of our phone conversations, "All grandparents who are raising grandchildren are grieving in one way or another." He is right. This isn't the kind of loss you get over quickly; it will take time and an acceptance of pain. Sometimes you feel like you're dancing as fast as you can, yet you continue to adapt to life's surprises.

WHAT WORKS

- Get to know your grandchildren's friends.
- Find out about income-based housing if necessary.
- Plan dates with your spouse and enjoy these special times.
- Get regular physical exams.
- Get medical insurance.
- Take care of yourself.

7

BUILDING A NEW LIFE TOGETHER

Stability is one of the best things you can give your grandchildren. Consistency, house rules, and unconditional love are the building blocks of stability. Providing a stable home will help your grandkids to see a future. Even better, your grandkids will believe they have a future. I put the list of our house rules on the refrigerator door. Several weeks later I took it down. By then, the twins probably knew every point by heart. Rules may change as children grow and mature, however.

HOUSE RULES MAY CHANGE

Once they turned 18 they were legal adults and could stay out as late as they pleased. Though we would go to bed, we didn't sleep well, and our grandparenting instincts were still active. We would wake up at 2 a.m. and ask, "Are the kids home yet?" Even if one twin was home we waited anxiously for the other. Interrupted sleep isn't restful sleep and the next day we looked and acted like sleep-deprived people.

I recall one sleepless night vividly. My grandson had come home, but my granddaughter was still out. After being awake for hours I finally drifted off to sleep. At 5:45 a.m., when I got up, I was shocked to see my granddaughter's bedroom door open and an empty bed. I couldn't believe my eyes so I peeked under the covers. No granddaughter. Suddenly, I recalled the terrible night my daughter died, the equally terrible night the twin's father died, and I began to panic.

Years had passed since these tragedies happened, yet my memories were vivid. Painful images, the same sights, sounds, colors and feelings, raced through my mind. I wondered if another tragic accident had happened and became increasingly anxious. Was I experiencing Post Traumatic Stress? Just as I was about to call the police my granddaughter walked in. "Where have you been?" I asked worriedly.

"Oh, we were watching a late-night movie and I fell asleep on Barb's couch," she replied. I asked my granddaughter why she hadn't called us. "I just woke up a few minutes ago," she explained. Her explanation was matter of fact, but my feelings weren't, and my anxiety lasted for hours. Some house rules had been dropped, but this incident reactivated one: Keep us informed. Most of the time the twins followed the rule and when they didn't we gave them a firm reminder.

Check your house rules. Are they still working? Do they need to be updated? Maybe the time has come to draw up new house rules. Give the idea some thought. Your grandchildren will be more apt to follow house rules if the rules change along with them. Some experts recommend regular family meetings. We tried this, but the meetings made the twins so uncomfortable we stopped.

GRIEF AND DEPRESSION AREN'T THE SAME

During the first months the twins lived with us we faced many challenges and one was sorting grief from depression. Anybody, even a grief counselor, would be depressed after two traumatic deaths. Though we expected the twins to have situational depression, we didn't know how long it would last. So we were on constant alert for mood swings, body language, and words that might indicate depression.

You may have asked yourself, "Is this grief or depression?" Dr. Kirsti A. Dyer charts the differences in her article, "Enhancing Well-Being by Understanding Grief and Taking a Loss History." Her chart lists key characteristics on the left, symptoms of grief in the middle, and symptoms of depression on the right. With grief, for example, vegetative signs disappear with time. With depression, vegetative signs persist two months after loss.

Energy level is another key characteristic. With grief, the person is agitated, restless and transient. With depression, the person's energy is persistently low or he or she has no energy at all. Mood is a characteristic that interests me. Grieving people have fluctuating moods, whereas depressed people feel consistently down. In time, and with lots of grief work, bereaved people come to terms with their loss and that's what the twins did.

Seek professional help if you think a grandchild is depressed. Depression is the most treatable of all mental illnesses and new medications have been developed. Your grandchild doesn't have to be miserable and you don't have to worry constantly.

Speaking of worry, you may be worried about yourself and think you're depressed. Life is dark and you don't think it will be bright again. Bob Deits addresses the depression issue in his book, *Life After Loss.* If you've been immobilized for weeks, or have no feelings at all, Deits says professional help is needed. "There is no shame in seeking help," he writes. "The only shame would be to need help and not get it."

SHARED ACTIVITIES

Planning shared activities with the twins is difficult because of our different interests and physical capabilities. We played Scrabble one evening and it was fun. However, it wasn't the kind of fun our grandchildren have with their aunt and a crowd of younger people. Our fun has physical limitations. My husband can still fish and hunt, for example, but he can't race up a hillside any more.

Try to include some fun in each day. What do you do for fun? What do your grandchildren do? You and your grandchildren may enjoy these shared activities.

- Visiting a science museum
- Going on a picnic
- Eating at the newest restaurant in town
- Watching a parade
- Exploring a street fair
- Ordering Chinese take-out or pizza
- Playing Frisbee
- Taking the dog for a walk
- Watching sailboats on a lake
- Going to a movie

- Raking leaves
- Putting up holiday decorations
- Baking cookies
- Riding bikes
- Canoeing

Ask your grandchildren for some additional ideas. Their suggestions could lead to many happy times together.

READING TO CHILDREN

Reading to children helps them in more ways than I can say. This can be a calming experience for babies, infants and toddlers. Preschoolers will learn the difference between real and pretend experiences and start to link sounds with alphabet letters. Stories also foster conversation between you and your grandchildren. To get a conversation going you might say, "I was worried about _____. Were you?"

Older grandchildren may expand their vocabularies. Reading stories to grandchildren increases their attention spans and makes them better listeners. Many public libraries have story hours for young children. The Rochester, Minnesota Public Library has put together reading kits for young children with eight to ten books in them. Parents read to the children or bring them to library story hours.

Recently my remaining daughter sent me an email about the books my husband and I read to her when she was little. To my amazement, she remembered the titles of the books, the main characters, and the plots. She sent the email to clarify memories of other stories. A few days later we talked on the phone. I mentioned a title she missed in her email. "Oh, I loved that story!" she exclaimed.

Your public library will be able to suggest titles of age-appropriate books for your grandchildren. The Oregon State University Extension Service has posted a list, "Children's Book List for Children Raised by Grandparents and/or Children Who Have Lost a Loved One." Visit www.exten-sion.oregonstate.edu/fch/sites/default/files/documents/ to read or print out the list. Grandparents' organizations may also be able to provide you with book titles.

ART HELPS KIDS HEAL

Since I minored in art in college and have a graduate degree in art, I'm an art booster. When our daughters were really young I bought them crayons and drawing paper. As they grew older we did art activities together, shrink art, which was popular at the time, decorating melamine plates, making clothespin people, drawing, painting, salt dough sculptures, sun catchers, and more.

During my teaching days my lesson plans were packed with art activities. I even had my nursery school students doing sand casting. Art helps children to recognize and accept their feelings. Art therapy does the same and more. What is art therapy? According to the American Art Therapy Association, it is a mental health profession that uses the creative process to "enhance the physical, mental and emotional well-being of individuals of all ages." Art therapists work in hospitals, hospices, schools, and privately.

You don't have to be a certified art therapist to help your grandchildren express themselves. I think grandchildren need to have new crayons, water color markers, age-appropriate scissors, water soluble glue, glue sticks, drawing paper, water color paper, a box of water colors, and colored paper. My daughters also enjoyed using stencils and rubber stamps. Watch for sales, especially just before school starts in the fall.

Your grandchildren should have a place to store their supplies. A plastic cleaning caddy with a handle is a good storage place and you can get them at discount stores for less than two dollars. Art supplies may also be stored in a desk drawer or kitchen drawer. Grandchildren should be able to use these supplies at any time. You may also take your grandchildren to an art museum or public art in your community.

GETTING PROFESSIONAL HELP

Grandchildren who live in grandparent-headed households may have been exposed to drug and alcohol behaviors. Some may have been given marijuana to keep them subdued. Others may have been exposed to crack labs. These children may have physical, emotional and mental problems. Worse, they may not trust adults and have no concept of consistency.

"Bad Habits/Annoying Behavior," an article on the University of Michigan Health System website, details a variety of problems. Hair twirling and pulling aren't just a problem, they can lead to loss of hair. For some, pulling hair is a self-calming behavior. Pulling hair from the scalp suggests a psychological problem that needs to be evaluated.

Your grandchildren may have tics, behaviors that are repeated over and over. Twitching eyes are an example. "Temporary tics are a habit that starts during childhood or the teen years, and might last anywhere from one month to a year," according to the article. Consult with a pediatrician if a grandchild's tics are getting worse.

Breath holding is one of the scariest behaviors for grandparents. Children have been known to hold their breath until they pass out. These spells usually happen when children are 18-24 months old. The problem with breath holding is that it can be seen as a seizure. If you've observed any breath-holding take your grandchild to the doctor.

Traumatized children, younger kids and teenagers, may develop ODD, Oppositional Defiant Disorder. These children are angry, argue all the time, and are blatantly defiant. An article about the disorder on the Family Doctor website lists the symptoms of ODD:

- Temper tantrums (They happen often.)
- Arguing with adults
- Ignoring rules and refusing to follow them
- Purposely annoying others
- Blaming others for their mistakes and behavior
- Feelings of anger and resentment
- Desire for revenge
- School problems
- Difficulty with making and keeping friends.

Interestingly, these same children may feel hurt easily. Medical researchers don't know the exact causes of ODD, but they know who is at risk for it. These children may be your grandchildren, who have a history of neglect, been exposed to violence and inconsistent discipline, and lack supervision. In order to diagnose ODD your physician will take a medical history, ask about family history, ask you to cite symptoms, and other problems you have witnessed. "Your doctor will probably work with another doctor who specializes in mental health," the article concludes.

Our granddaughter was in the car when her mother was mortally injured. We arranged for counseling and she attended the sessions for several months. Our grandson refused counseling and we respected his wishes, though we assured him it would always be available. Your grandchildren may need anger management training, grief counseling, or psychiatric counseling. A pediatrician should be able to give you more information on the types of counseling available. Social Services may also have information on counseling options.

PRACTICING PATIENCE

My husband and I had to be patient with our grandchildren and ourselves. We knew recovering from four deaths would take more time than recovering from one. Sometimes we went backwards on the recovery path. Still, our goal was to keep moving forward and help our grandchildren as much as possible. Patience and persistence are closely linked. The Zero to Three website, managed by the National Center for Infants, Toddlers, and Families, offers advice for dealing with frustrated children, the kids who need to learn patience.

The article, "Temperament: Persistence, Patience, and Frustration," says impatient and frustrated children (or grandchildren) tend to get upset the minute something goes wrong. This is understandable. Before they came to you, your grandchildren had some dark moments. Indeed, you may not know all they've been through. No wonder they get frustrated. No wonder they need to learn to trust again.

Patience will eventually pay off. According to the article, children who are persistent and learn patience are slower to "lose it" when they don't get their own way, and can tolerate waiting for their needs to be met." How can you practice patience with grandchildren? The article cites these tips and I have added personal comments.

- **Tell grandchildren what you're doing.** My granddaughter wanted to use the washing machine. The wash was done, but I hadn't put the load in the dryer because I had to stop this task in order to cook supper. We had just finished eating, so I said, "I'm cleaning up now and will be with you in a few minutes." Her answer: "I didn't mean to rush you, Grandma." What a sweet reply.
- **Sympathize and empathize.** Every conversation I have with my grandchildren is special to me. When they share information they are showing they trust me. I try to empathize and sympathize with them, without putting blame on others. "That would drive me crazy!" is an answer I often use.
- **Be a coach.** I'm not a coach in the true sense of the word, but have offered suggestions for the twin's research papers and reports. These suggestions include ways to make their work look better, such as a change in font and putting the paper in a colorful folder.
- **Divide big tasks into small parts.** Returning to university was a huge task for my grandson because he was moving into an apartment. To help him, I started gathering kitchen supplies and put the two boxes on the boot bench by the door. My checklist of kitchen

supplies was also helpful. He put a checkmark by the items that said "From Grandma" and bought the rest.

- **Diffuse the situation with humor.** Though my husband thinks I'm funny, I'm not sure the twins do. I have learned to laugh at myself and have been known to laugh so hard I have trouble stopping. "Grandma's losing it again," my grandson says.
- **Help grandchildren learn to pace themselves.** If the twins can't find me they know I'm downstairs writing in our home office. School supplies (extra tape, staples, page protectors, file folders, etc.) and gift wrapping supplies are stored there. One day my granddaughter needed something from the office. "I'm getting punchy!" I exclaimed. "It's time for a break." She smiled and nodded in agreement.
- **Be a role model.** You could call my husband Mr. Fixit because he can fix almost everything, car engines, washing machines, dryers, and vacuum cleaners. My grandson likes to fix things as well and is happiest when he's working on his car in the garage. Just before he went back to school he worked on his car and, though my husband could have helped him, he didn't. Instead, he provided tools, offered encouragement, and let our grandson do things for himself.

ACCEPTING GIFTS OF KINDNESS

I think of kindness as a gift, something you do to help another. In the last five years we have received many gifts of kindness. One family helped our daughter with gymnastics. Their daughter was on the team and they invited our

113

granddaughter for dinner before every practice session. Grief was still new and raw the first time our granddaughter went to their home. When she pulled up in front of the house, the entire family was waiting to welcome her.

"Everyone in the family, even their Grandma, was standing on the lawn. It was so sweet!" she exclaimed.

Family members continued to support us. We knew the first Thanksgiving without our daughter would be hard because she was born on Thanksgiving. To ease our pain, family members decided to have dinner at my niece's home. She and her husband had a hobby farm at the time and all of the children played with the goats, chickens, ducks and dogs. It was a Thanksgiving like no other in many ways.

The English novelist Joseph Conrad once said, "There is a kind way of assisting our fellow-creatures, which is enough to break their hearts while it saves their outer envelope." All of the gifts of kindness we have received exemplify his quote. These gifts were so generous, so helpful, we could have sobbed for days, yet they were in no way damaging. Rather, they were a tribute to our grandparenting efforts.

I'm sure you have received gifts of kindness as well. These gifts are comforting and, better yet, you may pass them on some day. Be sure to thank people for their gifts of kindness. I write thank-you notes (my mother trained me well), send an email thank-you, or send people one of my books. Some grandparents add these people's names to their prayer list.

EXPECTATIONS: YOURS AND THEIRS

The expectations we had for the twins reflected our value system: study hard, get an education, find a career you love, keep learning, and help others. Thankfully, our expectations didn't conflict with the twin's expectations. They came to us with the same value system, instilled by their mother and their extended family. Wow, we were lucky!

Children who have been emotionally harmed may have a survival-based value system. Teenagers may also have different values. These values change as they mature. Though we never really talked about the family value system, we were in sync. Our expectations for the twins were their expectations.

1. Attend school regularly.
2. Do your best.
3. Finish your homework.
4. Join afterschool activities.
5. Give to others (National Honor Society, community volunteer efforts).
6. Research a potential career.
7. Have fun.
8. Be respectful of others.
9. Do the right thing.
10. Connect with family.

Carl Pickhardt, PhD, examines expectations in his Psychology Today website article, "Surviving (Your Child's) Adolescence." Parents (and grandparents) should have a realistic set of expectations. These expectations can ease a child's way and help him or her to adjust. Having expectations doesn't mean you accept it when a child stops talking, stops doing schoolwork, or is dishonest, according to Pickhardt.

Middle school and high school students are capable of setting their own expectations. If your grandchildren are in fifth or sixth grade or any upper grades, you may wish to talk to them about their personal expectations. Write them down and compare their list with yours. How many matches do you see?

ONLINE COMMUNITIES AND BLOGS

Surf the Internet and you will find hundreds of grandparenting blogs. You can waste hours searching for a blog that meets your needs. Which one is best for you? A grandmother created a list you may find helpful, "The 50 Best Blogs by and About Grandparenting." This list is posted on many websites. Be aware, however, that it's a list by a grandmother, not a grandparent raising grandkids. You'll find more specific blogs in the section, "Internet Help for You" at the back of this book.

Before you post on a blog, I would read a dozen or so to get the tone of the website. Is this blog just a place for complaints? Does it offer tested tips from other GRGs and GAPs? When you find a blog you like, be careful about what you post. Your words will be on the Internet forever and you don't want them to come back and haunt you. As you write, remember that your job is to protect your grandchildren.

EVALUATING INTERNET ARTICLES

Internet articles often have snappy titles to get your attention. The snappy title doesn't necessarily represent a well-written, well-researched article. You need reliable information. To determine if an article is reliable, learn about the author's qualifications. Find out if the author is associated with a non-profit foundation, non-profit organization, or for-profit business. Check the main points, or assertions, in the article.

Dartmouth Medical School published a wallet card about evaluating assertions and I've adapted the points for this book.

1. What is the specific assertion? How many assertions are there in all?
2. If you think the assertion is true, would you care? Would the assertion alter your actions?
3. What individual, organization or business stands to benefit from the assertion?
4. Does the assertion have enough supporting evidence?
5. Does the author cite more than one study? How many studies are cited?
6. Have these studies been reviewed by peers?

You should also find out who is in charge of the website and pays the bills. See if you can find out when the website was last updated. Contact information should be readily available, not hidden in a small box or print that's hard to read.

WHAT WORKS

- Update house rules as grandchildren mature.
- Understand the differences between grief and depression.
- Plan activities you may share together.
- Read to children, including middle school kids.

- Let grandchildren express their feelings with art.
- Get professional help when necessary.
- Be patient with grandchildren and yourself.
- Thank others for their gifts of kindness.

8

FOSTERING CHILDREN'S GOALS AND DREAMS

I've written three nutrition activity books for children and many Internet articles about healthy eating. Long before I wrote these books I knew good food was brain food. When I use the term "good food" I'm referring to nutritious food and a balanced diet. Academic achievement hinges upon good food, normal servings, self-care, and enough sleep. For me, fixing nutritious, balanced meals for my grandchildren is a top priority.

Though I occasionally use mixes, I'm a made-from-scratch cook. I make my own sauces, soups (though I occasionally buy canned), muffins, and salad dressings. At our house, the favorite salad dressing is made with olive oil, rice vinegar, and Dijon mustard. "I love the dressing more than the salad!" my granddaughter exclaimed. The twins love this dressing so much both of them asked for the recipe.

GOOD FOOD IS BRAIN FOOD

The US Government is trying to get us to eat more fruits, vegetables and fiber. Your grandchildren also need to get enough calcium. We drink calcium fortified orange juice and skim milk. Low-fat cottage cheese is always available.

I always have seasonal fruit on hand, cherries, pears, apples, grapes, berries, oranges, tangerines and grapefruit. I use half white and half wheat flour for baking. Usually I make my own spaghetti sauce, though sometimes I add grated carrots and sliced mushrooms to a commercial brand.

Mealtimes bring people together and we expected the twins to eat dinner with us. Within a few months the twins were asking me to prepare their favorite dishes. Pasta Alfredo, made with skim milk, fat-free cream cheese and garlic, is one of my granddaughter's favorite meals. Both of the twins love my teriyaki-marinated flank steak. My grandson loves quiche, lasagna, roast beef "and anything with bacon." At dinner time I talked about avoiding high-salt foods and eating normal servings.

One of the best things you can do for your grandchildren is to teach them the difference between a portion and a serving. A portion is the amount of food you choose to eat, in other words, what you put on your plate. A serving is a measured amount of food based on nutrition data. Did you know the difference?

For more information about healthy eating visit the US Department of Agriculture website, http://www.choosemy plate.gov/ Your grandchildren may also track the food they eat by logging into the US Department of Agriculture Food Diary and Food Calorie Counter, http://www.livestrong. com/myplate/ If you don't have a computer your grandchildren may keep a food diary in a small notebook or blank book.

To foster learning and school success, make sure your grandchildren eat breakfast. Eating breakfast is like filling a car gas tank; it's fuel for the day. Sleepy, hurried grandchildren may want to bypass breakfast all together. Don't let them do it. Get the kids up earlier and make sure they eat breakfast that contains whole grains, fiber, and fruit.

Food is essential to physical and emotional survival. Bettyclare Moffatt makes this point in her book, *Soulwork.* She writes about her grandmother's fenced-off vegetable garden and the countless meals she prepared. Though her husband and sons died, her grandmother kept cooking and feeding others. "She fed her soul when she fed us," Moffatt writes. "She fed our souls too."

I am like her Texas grandmother. When I cook for my grandchildren I'm feeding my soul and theirs. At first, the meals we ate together were "fuel stops" and the twins ate quickly. Their eating pace slowed gradually and the twins began to linger after dinner. Our kitchen table became a healing place. Years passed and, after sharing hundreds of meals, we are a family, four people who share stories, laugh together, and say "I love you." It's a miracle.

SLEEPOVERS AND GETTING YOUR Zs

No matter how busy you are, no matter how stressed you feel, you still need to get a good night's sleep. Certainly, you don't want to slip into sleep deprivation. Mayo Clinic addresses this issue in a "Health Letter" article, "Sleep Deprivation: Not a Normal Part of Aging." While your sleep patterns change as you get older, the article says you don't have to "live with restless nights." Many factors affect sleep, including brain chemicals, the amount of light you're exposed to in a day, your diet, and alcohol consumption.

Fewer than five hours of sleep a night are insufficient, according to Mayo Clinic, and can increase your risk of falling by more than 50 percent. What are some other causes of poor sleep?

- A sleep disorder, such as leg cramps, obstructive sleep apnea, and restless legs
- The pain of heartburn, arthritis, back pain
- Frequent trips to the bathroom, especially if your take a diuretic
- Illness, such as a winter cold and coughing all night
- Medications that keep you awake, such as antidepressants
- Menopause
- Stress of caregiving
- Grief.

We eat earlier to get a better night's sleep. Instead of eating at six or 6:30 p.m. we now eat around 5:30 p.m., which gives us more time to digest food before bed time. Smaller servings also help us get the sleep we need. There are two streetlights in front of our house so we close the bedroom and bathroom doors. Even with closed doors we have enough light to find our way. The one thing we never, ever do is watch television in bed.

Both of my grandchildren like to sleep over at friends' houses and ask friends to sleep at our house. We bought a sleeper sofa for the lower level to foster sleepovers. I always have snacks on hand, though sometimes I've been caught short. It's a good idea to have an activity for kids, such as making pizza, watching a video series and playing computer games. Teenagers like to try new foods, and the sugar-free, low-fat ice cream sandwiches I bought were a hit.

Sleepovers can be sleepless nights for grandparents because the kids stay up for hours, making noise, running up and down stairs, and playing loud music. But sleepovers can also be times to share feelings, discuss problems, and find solutions and we need to give grandchildren opportunities to do these things.

As they drifted off to sleep I wanted my grandchildren to have comforting things around them. I hung two pictures in my grandson's bedroom. These weren't leftover pictures I found in a closet. Oh no, these pictures were chosen lovingly. One is a family photo, my husband and me, my brothers and sisters-in-law and my father-in-law. The other is a wildlife print. The photo is a reminder of family support. The wildlife print is a reminder of hunting with his father. I put a counted cross-stitch pillow in my granddaughter's room. Her mother gave it to me for my birthday many years ago and it's a beautiful example of her needlework skill. My granddaughter also has a photo of her mother and aunt with Pampa, my father-in-law. I took the photo, put it in a frame, and gave it to her for Christmas several years ago.

LEARNING TO LAUGH AGAIN

Laughter is Mother Nature's de-stressor, a way to relax for a few seconds or minutes. After four deaths in 2007 laughter eluded me; there just wasn't much to laugh about in my life. Thankfully, the twins said things that made me laugh. Laughter releases tension and brings people together. Sharing laughs with the twins makes me feel close to them.

You may have to give yourself permission to laugh. Laughing isn't a sign of disrespect or inappropriate behavior. Rather, it is a sign of a healthy spirit and a willingness to trust life again. My daughter was really funny. When I laugh I often think of her. Learning to laugh again will take some time. You can speed time along by being with upbeat friends, seeing humorous movies, and being alert to humor each day.

I made a conscious decision to avoid toxic people. You know the ones I mean. They're the people who always see the glass of life as half empty, never half full. Toxic people drag you down and squelch laughter, so it's best to avoid them. This can be hard if you see these people often, but maybe you can minimize your contacts with them. Be ready to laugh, for a good laugh can change your entire day.

YOUR HAPPINESS LINK

Remembering happy times can comfort grandchildren. To do this, your grandchildren need to x-out unhappy times for the moment and concentrate on happy times only. These remembrances help them to relax and let go of stress. Dr. Heidi Horsley and Dr. Gloria Horsley suggest another way to de-stress in their book, ***Teen Grief Relief.*** The technique, a Happiness Link, is simple and grandchildren may do it "anytime, anywhere, and no one will even know you're doing it."

To create a link you think of a happy thought, hold it in your mind, and at the same time, touch your index finger to your thumb to create a circle. I first heard about this technique when I was researching public speaking. The circle gesture is a way to diffuse tension before giving a presentation.

Your grandchildren may try this technique over and over again. Making a list of the "Top 10 Happiness Links" is also helpful, according to the Horsleys. I tried this and immediately thought of the time my in-laws met me in New Orleans the year my husband was stationed in Vietnam. While my mother-in-law watched the girls, my father-in-law and I went on a "date." As we were walking past a jazz bar the bouncer gave us a knowing look, a wink, and called, "Have a good time!"

Other Happiness Links include working at a church rummage sale with my daughter, sailing through a swarm of gnats with my brother, and visiting the Wabasha, MN Eagle Center with my former son-in-law. I also thought about the happiness associated with my grandchildren. The lists get longer as the twins get older. Here are some of the things that make me happy.

Granddaughter

- Hearing her sing along with CDs
- Her footsteps as she runs downstairs
- Compliments on my cooking
- Working hard on an assignment makes me think of her mother's persistence
- Smiles that light up her face

Grandson

- Hearing him whistling in the garage as he works on his car
- Food curiosity and appreciation

- His intellectual curiosity
- Seeing him plan dates with his girlfriend (My grandson knows every new restaurant, movie, and free event in town.)
- His protectiveness of his sister (Actually, they're mutually protective.)

You can make similar lists for your grandchildren. Thinking about these individualized lists made me appreciate my grandchildren even more. Young children will be able to make the circle gesture and talk about things that made them happy in the past. Older children are capable of making their own "Top 10" lists.

IMPORTANCE OF PLAY

Children learn by playing. Before your grandchildren came to live with you their play may have been limited. Make sure your grandchildren have time for original play, unstructured play created by them. Adults may join this play at the child's level. I often watched the twins when they were young. Since we hadn't cared for young children in a while we had some preparation work to do. My husband hung a swing from our back deck and started to build a wooden see-saw for the twins. Each Sunday, when they came for dinner, the twins checked the progress of his work. "Grandpa is building a park," my grandson said in a low, serious voice.

Our backyard is fairly steep and in the fall I showed the twins how to roll down the grassy bank. Since we're at the bottom of a hill, everyone on the block can see our yard. The neighbors must have thought I had "gone over the edge" and I pictured a couple peering out the window and talking about the scene.

Wife: "The poor dear. Harriet's finally lost it."
Husband: "What a shame."
Wife: "It happened quickly."
Husband: "Yep."

I hadn't lost it, I loved it and all of us had a marvelous time rolling down the hill. Fall had come and we could smell it in the air and hear it in the papery leaves as we rolled over them. As we rolled, more leaves fell from the giant 200-year old oak trees. After the twins grew tired of rolling, they raked leaves into piles. This memory, an example of original play with adult participation, is still clear in my mind and I can see the colors, smell the smells, and feel the joy of that day.

Original play is under attack, according to "Child's Play: Importance of Play Time for Children Neglected, Advocates Say," posted on The Town Talk website. "Since the 1970s, kids have lost an average nine hours of free play-time a week," the article asserts. Worse, children are getting less free time outside. Nine hours a week multiplied by 52 weeks a year equals 468 hours a year, hours of joyful learning lost forever.

This fact reminds me of a conversation I had with my sister-in-law. She and her husband used to live on a hillside overlooking a flat stretch of land in the valley below. They were concerned when a developer bought the land, laid out blocks, paved the streets, and started building dozens of houses. "We thought the sound from below would be disruptive," she noted, "but we never heard a sound and never saw a child. All of the parents were working." What a sad commentary on modern life.

Today, the world is a more dangerous place and parents can't be blamed for worrying about their children's safety. Parents can't be blamed for worrying about their kids spending hours at the mall or driving the family car. Play helps grandchildren to solve problems, make decisions, learn new words, build relationships, and handle disappointments. I think original play helps a child to create an identity that stays with him or her throughout life. There are many other benefits as well, according to an article, "The Importance of Original Play in Human Development," posted on the Playing By Heart website.

Original play reduces fear, anxiety, stress and irritability, the article explains, and is a healing process for children's hurts. Social benefits include sharing, compassion, and empathy. This kind of play increases a child's range of motion, coordination, balance and fine motor skills. According to the article, original play also increases the efficiency of brain function. As a GRG or GAP your job is to foster original play and keep children safe.

Though you join in the play at the child's level, let your grandchildren guide their play and add dialogue. Pay attention to what they are saying and doing. Instead of hurrying things along, let the play evolve and develop at its own pace. If you need to interrupt for safety reasons, be gentle and speak in a calm voice. "You are the most important play equipment," the article concludes.

CREATIVE OUTLETS

Child life experts understand the importance of creative outlets. Whether it is drawing, painting, sculpture, singing, acting, dancing, or other outlets, creative experiences help children to express feelings. These outlets may also diminish emotional outbursts. Stanford University describes the values of these outlets in a website article by Patti Kahn, "Healing HeARTS: Packard Children's Program Offers Creative Outlet to Sick Kids."

The article describes an art show at the Lane Medical Library, a collection of 22 art works by ill children. Below her drawing of flowers and stuffed animals one 14-year-old wrote, "Recovery is possible." A 10-year-old boy described his drawing of a sailboat and illness journey with a single sentence: "I am a pirate ship in a storm." Grace Cheng, MD, a Packard Children's general pediatric hospitalist and medical school instructor, established the Healing HeARTS program.

Grandchildren don't have to be ill in order to benefit from healing arts. School-age children may participate in concerts, plays, and art exhibits. A grandchild who is interested in acting may participate in children's theater. Toddlers can express their feelings with scribble drawings, named scribbles, play dough, singing, dancing, and puppetry.

Photography is my granddaughter's creative outlet and she won top prizes at the Minnesota State Fair and our county fair. We did everything we could to encourage this outlet, loaning her cameras, lenses, delivering and picking up contest submissions. This interest in photography continues to this day and her photos are astonishing. You can foster a similar interest by buying a disposable camera for a child or loaning him or her a camera.

If you think a grandchild is exceptionally talented, you may wish to look into private lessons. Scouting programs may also provide training. A local artist or business may be willing to provide free lessons.

Our granddaughter participated in a high school mentoring program and received free training from a local photographer. Our grandson was interested in learning how to play his father's guitar, a vintage instrument that turned out to be quite valuable. The guitar linked him with his father and we gave him guitar lessons for Christmas. Though he didn't take lessons for long, he had the satisfaction of using his father's guitar and making music.

GOAL--SETTING IS A SIGN OF PROGRESS

Okay, let's get real. You're feeling swamped, you wonder if you're going to make it, and hope you're making progress with your grandchildren. With all that you have to do, there's one more thing to add to the list and it's helping grandchildren to set goals. Why should you bother? Goal-setting is a sign of hope, a belief that life will get better, and you need to nurture this belief.

The ability to set goals and work towards them is similar to planting seeds.

Seeds are symbols of hope. You plant seeds because you think they will grow. Daniel Goleman writes about the link between goals and hope in his book, *Emotional Intelligence: Why it Can Matter More than IQ.* The ability to have hope means you won't give in to overwhelming anxiety, self-defeating thoughts, depression, or the set-backs of life, according to Goleman. "People who are hopeful evidence less depression than others as they maneuver through life in pursuit of their goals," he writes.

But your grandchildren's lives have been disrupted and setting goals is hard for them. That doesn't mean goal-setting is impossible. Usually goal-setting begins with objectives. Your grandchildren may be so stressed they can't think of any objectives, so I recommend starting with one. It's helpful to do this on paper.

1. What is my goal?
2. Why is it important?
3. Is the goal reasonable?
4. What steps do I need to take?

Goal-setting resources say you should set a deadline for each. Setting a deadline now may be too much pressure for your grandchild and you can skip this step if necessary. Still, your grandchild may continue to work towards this goal. Pepperidge Farm created a Fishful Thinking website to help "parents raise children who have a positive attitude and can confidently tackle life's challenges." Dr. Karen Reivich, a psychology professional and mother of four, helped to establish the site and it focuses on five issues: optimism, emotional awareness, goal setting/hope, resilience, and empowerment. The site warns visitors when an Ad Nooze, or advertisement, is coming. Go to http://www.fishfulthinking.com for more information about goal-setting. (In mentioning this website I am not endorsing Pepperidge Farm products.) Goal-setting worksheets are also available on the Internet.

Much as I hate to say this, I think one of my granddaughter's goals, reaching a height of five feet, isn't possible even with gymnastics and growth spurts. By today's standards, my husband and I are short people and their parents were shorter than most. She has short genes (no pun on words intended). This fact has not escaped her notice. In fact, it has made her stronger, a woman of high standards and convictions. When I think of the twin's physical attributes I think of a friend's favorite saying, "small but mighty."

REACHING GOALS TAKES TEAM EFFORT

While children may reach goals without adult assistance, you can ease the way for them. Knowing you are rooting for them will give your grandchildren energy and hope. As soon as a grandchild sets a goal you're automatically a member of his or her team. Do all you can to help your grandkids reach their goals. Your participation may include car-pooling, buying supplies and hosting sleepovers.

The high school my grandchildren attended fostered group projects, work done by five or six students, summarized in a written report. "Can my group spend the night, grandma?" she asked. "We have to finish our project and write a report." Of course I said yes and six giggling girls showed up a few hours later. We had to move the ping pong table aside to make room for all of their sleeping bags. The girls worked well into the night.

This was team effort in action. Though grandchildren may receive help from friends, you are still on their team, part of a family effort to help them set goals and reach them. Once they have achieved these goals it will be time to set new ones.

You may also set new goals for yourself. "I will be less over-protective," I vowed and kept this promise.

BALLOONS: CHARTING PROGRESS

This summer I attended the national conference of The Compassionate Friends, an organization for parents and families that have lost a child. I participated in a panel discussion, autographed books in the conference book store, and talked with people about my forthcoming book about finding happiness after loss. To build interest in the book I displayed a mini poster and put out a sign-up sheet. "How do you know you're happy?" someone asked.

Talk about a pithy question! Details raced through my mind and, since giving her a complete answer would take at least an hour, I talked about the twin's accomplishments. "These results make me happy," I concluded. Later, I mentioned this conversation to Dr. Gloria Horsley, one of the founders of The Compassionate Friends. "I wasn't quite sure how to answer the question," I admitted.

"Think about where you were before," she suggested, "and think about where you are now."

No doubt about it, the contrast was startling and exciting, as exciting as hot air balloons in flight. One balloon represents the formation of a new family. Another represents the twin's accomplishments. Yet another represents their successful college searches, admissions, and making the Dean's List. Recent celebration balloons would be the ability to talk about feelings and say, "I love you."

Think about the celebration balloons in your life. Compare the past with the present to see how far you've come. A grandchild may have become calmer, for example, or start to joke with you. An irresponsible grandchild may be more responsible now. Your grandchildren may have grown taller and look healthier. All of these things are rewards for being a GRG or GAP. All of these things make you happy.

LETTING GO AGAIN

I let go of my daughters long ago. Never in my wildest dreams did I think I would have to let go of my grandchildren, but my husband and I are slowly doing it. The twins wanted to search for colleges on their own, not with us, and we went along with the idea. Searching for a college was easier for my grandson because he had only one choice. My granddaughter was different. She started with five choices, narrowed them down to two, and finally one.

Though we tried to stay uninvolved with the college search, we were able to nudge our grandchildren in directions we thought were best for them. I was proud of our grand-parenting, even prouder when we didn't cry when we took the twins to their respective colleges. Leave-taking was a bit harder this year. Having the twins home for the summer was so much fun that I didn't want the fun to end. "I'll probably cry," I blurted.

"Don't do that Grandma," my granddaughter cautioned. I assured her I wouldn't.

The twins are 20 years old now and I have to let go of them more. "Letting go" is a term that is usually associated with the death of a family member or friend, a time when the survivor begins to release emotional ties. Bob Deits, in his book *Life After Loss*, says we will never regain the balance in our lives unless we let go. As he writes, "This letting go of the past is crucial to moving on to a future after your loss."

Has the time come for you to let go? Maybe you need to let go of disappointment. You may need to let go of anger. Like me, you may need to let go of sorrow. Letting go is a slow process, one you need to experience for yourself and grandchildren. When you let go, you're not getting go of love. You're letting go **because** of the love you have for your grandchildren. This thought comforted me and I hope it comforts you.

ARE YOU STILL YOU?

Life has changed so dramatically you may feel like you've lost yourself. "Who am I now?" you ask. Don't worry. The talents, education and experience you had before you started raising your grandchildren are still part of you. Instead of losing your identity you have expanded it. Today, you are the new and improved model of yourself.

Raising grandchildren changes your view of the world. You have expectations for your grandchildren. Dreams for the future pop into your head at odd times. Looking ahead, you see a time when your grandchildren have their children and wonder how they will look. Often my husband and I talk about the energy, laughter and experiences the twins bring to our lives.

Katrina Kenison makes some important points in her book, *The Gift of an Ordinary Day.*

She describes the fast pace of her life. "Lately, I've noticed that when someone asks me how I'm doing, I reply by telling them how busy I've been." This sentence startled me because I have done the same thing. A balanced life has a rhythm, according to Kenison, and she goes on to say "a thoughtful life is not rushed." Before I read her book I came to the same conclusion and slowed my thoughts.

Slowing my thoughts didn't mean I was slow in general. I continued to write, but more thoughtfully, I continued to work on daily tasks, only more thoughtfully. When I slowed my thoughts I became more aware of the strengths I brought to grandparenting. Stop reading for a few moments and think about the strengths that you bring to this role, and the love that sustains you. In the end, life is all about love.

IT'S ALL ABOUT LOVE

Accepting our GRG roles was easy for my husband and me. This role came from love and we would fulfill it with love. The love we have for the twins has buoyed us through hard times and keeps us going. Several friends have asked me if we visit our daughter's grave often. We don't. Loving and raising her children is our memorial to our daughter and former son-in-law. The question made me curious, however, and one day I asked my grandson if he had visited the gravesite.

He answered without hesitation. "Once." His mother and father are buried side-by-side and he visited the site with the man our daughter had planned to marry.

Some grandparents aren't very close to their grandchildren. Becoming a GRG or GAP gives you opportunities to know and love them, not spoil them, but love them. Love is also a source of courage, according to Judy Tatelbaum. She makes this point in her book, ***The Courage to Grieve*** and says we can practice being courageous. "Having the courage to grieve leads to having the courage to live, to love, to risk, and enjoy all the fruits of life without fear or inhibition."

I practiced being courageous and, just as Tatelbaum predicts, I became courageous. Your experiences may be similar to mine. Love can lead us and take us to where we need to go. Years from now, your grandchildren may not remember experiences clearly, but they will remember your love. It really is the tie that binds.

WHAT WORKS

- Eat dinner together as a family.
- Know the difference between a portion and a serving.
- Keep the television out of the bedroom.
- Laugh with your grandchildren and at yourself.
- Create Happiness Links.
- Play with grandchildren.
- Foster creative outlets.
- Help children set and achieve goals.

Conclusion

Becoming a GRG has been the most meaningful journey of my life. It has been the greatest challenge as well. While I was grieving for four family members, I had to protect and nurture two vulnerable kids. No wonder there were times when I felt like I was on emotional overload. Fortunately, I recognized these times and took steps to maintain my physical and mental health. Still, it wasn't easy.

Writing this book has also been another journey and I wouldn't have been able to do it without my husband's support. We started our marriage as a team and we are still a team. Again, I thank Rabbi Earl A. Grollman for his kindness, encouragement, and phone calls. I am grateful to Kenneth J. Doka, PhD for writing the Foreword. And I can't thank Dr. Robert Veninga enough for his back cover review.

Raising grandchildren changed my life and it will change yours. Many exciting and loving experiences await you if your journey has just begun. If you have been raising grandchildren for years I salute you. For you, the benefits of this role are apparent. Here are some of the benefits and you may think of more.

- You are helping a vulnerable child or children.
- Unlike grandparents who live far away, you see your grandchildren all the time and know them.

- Thanks to you, grandchildren are growing and learning and becoming.
- You are helping to sustain family values.
- Your grandchildren are safe and out of harm's way.
- Grief and pain have given you a greater appreciation of life.
- Each morning you awaken with a sense of purpose.
- Becoming a GRG or GAP has made you a stronger person.
- The house is filled with energy, sound, and laughter.
- When you go to sleep at night you can say, "I'm making a difference."
- You're giving grandchildren a role model for the future.
- Last, and far from least, you have experienced miracles, the smiles, trust and love of a child.

Our society isn't very kind to older people and age has worked against me many times. Not this time. Age and experience are working for me. From idea to reality, the twins knew I was writing this book. In fact, they helped me with word processing. When I started the book I promised there would be nothing harmful within its pages, and I've kept this promise. Though I've told stories about them, these stories don't contain any hurtful ideas or words; they are family stories, accounts to be told and retold.

To my knowledge, I have made only one hurtful comment since the twins came to live with us. The comment: "We're getting too friendly with the police." A visit from two police officers with guns drawn, a late-night phone call, and my grandson's speeding ticket were enough for me. The speeding ticket was dismissed later, yet I think my comment was well-founded.

Before I became a GRG I thought I was a strong person. I'm far stronger now. This strength has become part of my life, my thinking, and problem-solving abilities. The other day, as I was checking out of a discount store, the sales associate asked, "Do you have any coupons?"

"No," I answered. "I'm not that smart."

"I'm street smart!" the young man exclaimed.

"Well, I'm grandma smart," I replied, "and a force to be reckoned with."

"Woo!" he said with surprise.

We are a force to be reckoned with and our power is growing. While there is a network of GRGs and GAPs in the nation, it needs to be better connected. The bolts need to be tightened and you can help. Reach out to other grandparents who are raising their grandkids. Take advantage of grandparenting resources. Visit and learn from Internet blogs and websites. Please visit my website, www.harriethodgson. com, click on the blog tab at the top, and post your thoughts. You are also welcome to send an email to harriethodgson@ charter.net.

Our grandchildren, yours and mine, bring energy and new ideas to our lives. They come to us with a special gift and it is a gift of hope. In time, we have hope for our grandchildren, hope for our family, hope for ourselves, and hope for the future. Life is wonderful!

Grandparent's Bill of Rights

Grandparents who are raising their grandchildren have many rights. You have the right to:

- Enjoy your grandchildren.
- Feed them nutritious, balanced meals and normal servings.
- Give your grandkids sandwiches if they reject dinner.
- Make play part of each day.
- Help with homework, but don't provide answers.
- Teach grandchildren basic manners.
- Ask grandchildren to help around the house.
- Laugh at your own jokes even if they're sappy.
- Ask permission to give grandchildren hugs.
- Expect teens to provide who, what, when, where, why and how details.
- Set reasonable bedtimes and curfews.
- Use the word no, when necessary.
- Teach grandkids how to budget and save money.
- Get grandkids to clean up their bedrooms and ignore the "moanie-groanies."
- Require drivers to fill the car gas tank when gauge reads one quarter full.

- Ask grandkids to turn the car radio back to your favorite station.
- Stop loud music and phone calls after 9 p.m.
- Repeat stories even if your grandchildren roll their eyes.
- Say "I love you" every day.

Internet Help For You

- Administration on Aging, www.aoa.gov/prof/notes/Docs/ Grandparents_Raising_Grandchildren.pdf
- AARP (American Association of Retired Persons) Grandparent Information Center, www.aarp.org/families/ grandparents
- American Academy of child and Adolescent Psychiatry, www.aacap.org
- American Bar Association Center for Children and Law, www.abanet.org/child/home.html
- American Psychological Association, www.apa.org
- Creative Grandparenting, www.creativegrandparenting.org
- Christian Legal Society, www.clsnet.org
- Grandparent Caregivers: A National Guide, http://www. igc.org/justice/cjc/lspc/manual.cover.html
- Grandparenting Foundation, www.grandparenting.org
- Grandparents as Parents, http://home1.gte.net/res02wo7
- Grandparents Resource Center, http://grc4usa.org
- Grandparents Who Care, www.grandparentswhocare.com
- Intergenerational Connections, http://www.nnfr.org/igen
- National Center for Grandparents Raising Grandchildren, www.chhs.gsu.edu/nationalcenter
- National Legal Aid & Defender Association, www.nlada.org
- Social Security Benefits for Grandchildren, www.ssa/gov/ kids/parents5.htm

- The American Self-Help Clearinghouse, www.selfhelp-groups.org
- The Compassionate Friends, www.tcf.org
- The Foundation for Grandparenting, www.grandparenting.org
- The Grandparents Rights Organization, www.grandparentsrights.org
- The Open to Hope Foundation, www.opentohope.com
- USA Government blog, www.usa/gov/Topics/Grandparents.shtml
- US Government Housing Assistance, www.housingassistanceonline.com

Words To Know

accumulated loss – stored, buried loss that flares unexpectedly and without warning

adoption – termination of parental rights; grants all rights and obligations for the care of a child to another relative, including grandparents

anniversary reaction – feelings of loss and grief sparked by a date, event, or experience

anticipatory grief – feeling of loss before a death or dreaded event occurs

art therapy – using art and the creative process to treat psychiatric and psychological conditions

caregiver – person who cares for another's needs, health and well-being

conservator – legal designation given to an adult granting him or her the right to manage a minor's finances; requires extensive reporting to the court

creative outlets – variety of art experiences of healthy and ill children

depersonalization – watching life from the outside without being personally involved

depression – feeling of despondency and pessimism about the future; a medical illness

denial – conscious or unconscious refusal to accept facts

diary – a written daily record of your activities and thoughts

emotional vocabulary – having enough words to express feelings

family caregiver – family member who cares for another either short-term or long-term

foster parent – individual who acts as a parent or guardian in place of a child's natural parents; is not legal adoption

grandfamily – merging of grandparents and grandchildren into a family unit

grief – a natural response to loss; varies with the individual

grief reconciliation – acceptance of loss and returning to life

GAP – grandparent as parent

GRG – grandparent raising grandchildren

guardian – designation given to an adult granting him or her the responsibility for a minor's life

idealization – form of denial in which the bereaved remembers only the good things about the deceased; may include exaggeration

journal – a regularly written record of your activities, thoughts and ideas; may also be daily

kinship care – grandparent or other relative caring for a child

legal custody – grandparent asks for legal custody of grandchild or grandchildren because the parents are unfit

letting go – a process of developing emotional detachment from a deceased loved one or living person

linking object – an object that links an individual with a deceased or absent person, such as a watch

loss history – written record of a person's losses to date

magical thinking – preschooler's tendency to mix reality with fantasy

Memo for Record – a written record containing dates, events, and concerns; may be used in a court of law

multiple losses – many or successive deaths; requires longer recovery time than the loss of an individual

peer group – an influential group of people usually of similar age

power of attorney – allows grandparents to make decisions regarding a child's welfare; does not involve transference of legal custody

ODD (Oppositional Defiant Disorder) – angry, defiant, argumentative behavior in excess of what is normal for children and teens

original play – non-structured play for children; adults may participate at the child's level of development

Post Traumatic Stress Disorder (PTSD) – a pattern of symptoms following a traumatic event; symptoms include anxiety, tensions, nightmares and depression

relative foster care – grandchild or grandchildren are placed in the legal custody of the state, but live in the grandparent's home or another relative's home

self-care – steps taken by an individual to feel better

situational depression – temporary depression caused by a specific event or events

stressor – any upsetting change that has physical or emotional outcomes

projection – attributing one's own traits, attitudes and faults to others

traumatic death – sudden and unanticipated loss; frequently violent, random or preventable

value system – standards accepted by an individual or society; desirable achievements

Worth Reading

Adcox, Susan. "Asian Grandparents Have Influence, Status," posted on the About.com website, http://grandparents.about/com/od/grandparentingtoday/a/Asian grandparents.htm

Adcox, Susan. "Grandparents as Parents: GRGs/GAPs Have Major Issues to Resolve," posted on the About.com website, http://grandparents.about.com/od/grandparenting issues/tp/RaisingGrand.htm.

Adcox, Susan. "When Grandparenting Isn't Fun," posted on the About.com website, http://grandparents.about.com/od/grandparentingissues/a/GrandparentIssues.htm

Al-Azami, Dr. Salman and Gyllenspetz, Ian. "Grandparents and Grandchildren: Learning Together," www.grandparentsplus.org.uk/wp-content/uploads/2011/03/Schools, p. 1–13.

Allen, David M, MD. "A Matter of Personality: From Borderline to Narcissism," posted on the Psychology Today website, http://www.psychologytoday.com/blog/matter-personality/201106/grandparents-raising-gr

American Academy of Child & Adolescent Psychiatry. "Grandparents Raising Grandchildren," posted on the AACAP website, http://www.aacap.org/cs/root/facts.

American Art Therapy Association. "The Association's Mission," http://arttherapy.org/aata-aboutus.html

American Association for Marriage and Family Therapy. "Grandparents Raising Grandchildren," posted on the AAMFT website, http://www.aamft.org.imis15/content/ consumer updates/Grandparents Raising Grandchild.

Bales, Diane. "Grandparents Raising Grandchildren: Helping Grandchildren Stay in Contact with Parents," University of Georgia website, www.fcs.uga.edu/pubs/PDF/ CHFD-E-59-2.pdf, p. 3–4.

Barauski, Sue, et al. "Involving Immigrant and Refugee Families in Their Children's Schools: Barriers, Challenges and Successful Strategies." Washington, DC: US Department of Health and Human Services, p. 1.

Berman, Diane, PsyD, PCPC. "Supporting Your Teenager Through Grief and Loss," "Bethesda Special Needs Parents Examiner," http://www.examiner.comspecial- needs-parents-in-washington-dc/supporting-your-teenager

Bolton, Robert, PhD. *People Skills: How to Assert Yourself, Listen to Others, And Resolve Conflicts.* New York: Simon & Schuster, 1986, p. 4–5, 32-39, 55, 59, 143.

Borba, Michele, EdD. "Hot Homework Tips for Parents: Ways to Minimize Our Nagging and Maximize Their Learning," posted on the Parenting Bookmark website, http:// www.parentingboookmark.conm/pages/articleMB05.htm.

Cancer.Net. "Helping a Child or Teenager Who is Grieving," American Cancer Society website, www. cancer.net/patient/Copoing/Grief+and+Bereavement/ Helping+Grieving+Children.

Chicago Tribune Homes website. "Grandparents Raising Grandchildren," http://www.chicagotribune.com/classified/ reslestate/chi-primetime-grandparent-0226110

Coffey, Laura T. "10 Tips for Grandparents Raising Grandchildren: How to Avoid Financial Shipwreck When Raising Your Children's Children," posted on the Today website, http://today/msnbc.com/id/16876875/ns/today-money/t/tips-grandparents-raising-grand

Concept to Classroom. "Why are Afterschool Programs Good for School-Age Children and Youth," posted on the Concept to Classroom website, http://www.thirteen.org/edonline/concept2class/afterschool/index_sub3.html

Cornell University. "Role Changes/Transitions: Grandparents Raising Grandchildren," posted on the Cornell website, www.cornellcares.org/pdf/handouts/rct_grand parents.pdf.

Dannison, Linda, PhD, CFLE and Smith, Andrea B., PhD, LSW. "Understanding Emotional Issues in Your Grandchildren's Lives," posted on the Family Information Services website, www.wmich/edu/grs/forms/understanding-emotional-issues.pdf

Daily Strength Blog. "Our Son Hates Us Now," http://www.dailystrength.org/c/Grandparents_Raising_Grandchildren/forum/12617395-our-son-

Dartmouth Medical School, Center for the Evaluative Clinical Sciences. "Evaluating an Assertion" wallet card.

Davies, Curt and Williams, Dameka. "Lean on Me: Support and Minority Outreach for Grandparents Raising Grandchildren," published on the AAP website, www.aarp.org/relationships/grandparenting/info-2003/aresearch-import-483.html, Part 1, page 8, Part 2, p. 39-45.

Daykin, Tom. "Kid-Friendly Senior Housing Proposed," published in the "Journal Sentinel," http://www.jsonline.com/realestate/39170862.html

Diets, Bob, M. Th. *Life After Loss: A Practical Guide to Renewing Your Life After Experiencing Major Loss.* Cambridge, MA: Lifelong Books, 2004, p. 50-51, 60, 124–128, 216.

Dyer, Kirsti A., MD, MS. FAAETS, FACW, NCBF, CWS. "Enhancing Well-Being By Understanding Grief & Taking a Loss History," posted on the Medical Wellness Archives website, http://www.medicalwellnessassociation.com/articles/grief.htm.

Family Doctor Editorial Staff. "Oppositional Defiant Disorder," published on the Family Doctor website, http://familydoctor.org/online/famdocen/home/common/mental health/kids/953.html

Family Education Website. "Perfecting the Art of the Compliment,"http://life.familyeducation.com/compliments/communication-skills/48978.html

Fay, Jim and Cline, Foster W., MD. *Grandparenting with Love & Logic.* Golden, CO: The Love and Logic Press, Inc., 1994, p. 62, 134–135, 185

Ferrer-Chancy, Millie, Forthun, Larry F. and Falcone, Angela. "Grandparents Raising Grandchildren; Building Strong Families," posted on the University of Florida Extension website, http://edis/ifas.ufl.edu, p. 2.

Ferrer-Chancy, Millie, Forthun, Larry F., Falfone, Angela, and Pergola, Joe. "Grandparents Raising Grandchildren: Understanding Relationships," posted on the University of Florida Extension website, http://edis.ifas.ufl.edu.fv435.

Frank, Christina. "The Need for Parenting Consistently," posted on the Parenting website, http://www.parenting.com/article/the-need-for-consistency

Gaillard, Kathy. "More African American Parents are Raising Grandchildren," posted on the "National Grandparents Raising Grandchildren Examiner" website, http://www.examiner.com/grandparents-raising-grandchildren-in-national/more-african-am

Goleman, Daniel. *Emotional Intelligence: Why it Can Matter More Than IQ*. New York: Bantam Books, 1997, p. 87.

Goyer, Amy. "More Grandparents Raising Grandkids: New Census Data Shows an Increase in Children Being Raised by Extended Family," posted on the AARP website, http://www.aarp.org/relationships/grandparenting/info-12-2010/more_grandparents_raising

Grandparents Weekly website. "Tax Tips for Grandparents Raising Grandchildren," http://www.parenting weely.com/grandparents/tax tips.htm

Grief Speaks website. "Teen Grief in School," http://www.griefspeaks.com/id36.html

Grohol, John M, PsyD. "5 Secrets to a Successful Long-Term Relationship or Marriage," posted on the PsychCenter website, http://psychcentra.com/lib/2007/5-secrets-to-a-successful-long-term-relationship-or-marria

Grollman, Earl A. *Straight Talk about Death for Teenagers: How to Cope with Losing Someone You Love*. Boston: Beacon Press, 1993, p. 33.

Horsley, Dr. Heidi and Horsley, Dr. Gloria. *Teen Grief Relief: Parenting with Understanding, Support and Guidance*. Highland City, FL: Rainbow Books, 2007, p. xix, xx, 49.

Kahn, Patti. "Healing HeARTS: Packard Children's Program Offers Creative Outlet to Sick Kids," posted on the Stanford University website, http://news.stanford.edu/news/2006/february8/med-art-020806.html

Kenison, Katrina. *The Gift of an Ordinary Day: A Mother's Memoir.* New York: Grand Central Publishing, 2009, p. 253–255.

Laden, Meredith. "Understand The Five Essentials Children Need from Parents," posted on the Bright Hub website, http://www.brighthub/com/parenting/grade-school/articles/62715.aspx

LiveStrong website. "List of Life Skills Children Should Have," http://www.livestrong.com/article/125579-list-life-skills-children-should/

Mayo Clinic writers. "Sleep Deprivation: Not a Normal Part of Aging," "Mayo Clinic Health Letter," September 2011, p. 6.

Minkler, Meredith, Dr. Fuller-Thompson, Esme, PhD, Miller, Doriane, MD, Driver, Diane, PhD. "Depression in Grandparents Raising Grandchildren," "Archives of Family Medicine," Volume 6, September/October, 11997, p. 445–452.

Moffatt, Bettyclare. *Soulwork: Clearing the Mind, Opening the Heart, Replenishing the Spirit.* Berkeley, CA: Wildcat Canyon Press, 1994, p. 36.

National AfterSchool Association Code of Ethics, www.naaweb.org, p. 3-15.

Noel, Brook and Blair, Pamela D., PhD. *I Wasn't Ready to Say Goodbye: Surviving, Coping & Healing After the Sudden Death of a Loved One.* Milwaukee, WI: Champion Press, Ltd., 2000, p. 84-89.

Ohio State University Extension. "Grandparents as Parents Again," posted on the Ohio State University website, http://ohioline.osu.edu/ss-fact/0157.html

Original Play website. "The Importance of Original Play in Human Development," http://www.originalplay.com/develop.htm

Oregon State University Extension Service. "Children's Book List for Children Raised by Grandparents and/or Children Who Have Lost a Loved One," posted on the Oregon State University website, www.extension.oregonstate.edu/fch/sites/default/files/documents/

Pickhardt, Carl, PhD. "Surviving (Your Child's) Adolescence," posted on the Psychology Today website, http://www.psychologytoday.com/blog/surviving-your-childs-adolescense/201003/adolesce

Poe, Lenora M. "Connecting the Bridges: Grandparenting Children," posted on the University of Wisconsin website, http://parenthood.library.wisc.edu?poe/poe.html.

Ransford, Marc. "Grandparents More Loving, Strict When Raising Youngsters," posted on the Ball State University web-site, http://www.bsu.edu/news/article/0.1370.-1019-272.00.html.

Reynolds, Glenda Phillips, Wright, James V. and Beale, Betty. "The Roles of Grandparents in Educating Today's Children," "Journal of Instructional Psychology," Dec. 2003, p. 2.

Ross, Maisie, Forthun, Larry F., Ferrer-Chancy, Millie and Falcone, Angela. "Grandparents Raising Grandchildren: Health Care Assistance," posted on the University of Florida website, http://edis.ifas.ufl.edu/fy1123

Strom, Robert D. and Strom, Shirley K. "Meeting the Challenge of Raising Grandchildren," "International Journal of Aging and Human Development," Volume 51, p. 185–186.

Tannen, Deborah, PhD. *That's Not What I Meant! How Conversational Style Makes or Breaks Relationships*. New York: Ballantine Books, 1986, p. 39, 122, 180.

Tatelbaum, Judy. *The Courage to Grieve: Creative Living, Recovery & Growth Through Grief*. New York: Harper & Row, Publishers, Inc., 1980, p. 10, 31.

Teach Kids How website. "How to Give and Receive a Compliment," http://www.teachkidshow.com/how-to-give-and-receive-a-compliment/

The Town Talk website. "Child's Play: Importance of Play Time for Children Neglected, Advocates Say," http://www.the-towntalk.com/article/20110823/LIFESTYLE/108230306/Child-s-Play-Impor

Tousley, Marty, CNS-BC, FT, DCC. "Persistent Dreams in Grief," posted on the Open to Hope Foundation website, http://www.opentohope.com/?post=persistent-dreams-in-grief

Tremblay, K. R., Jr., Barber, CD and Kubin, L. "Grandparents: As Parents," posted on the Colorado State University Extension website, http://www.ext.colostate.edu/pubs/consumer/10241.html

University of Michigan Health System. "Bad Habits/Annoying Behavior," posted on the University of Michigan Health System website, http://www.med/umich.edu/yourchild/otpics/badhabit.html

US Department of Education. "Homework Tips for Parents," published on the ED.gov website, http://www2.ed.gov/pring/parents/academic/involve/homework/part.html

Valeo, Tom. "Strategies for Happiness: 7 Steps to Becoming a Happy Person," published on the webMD website, http://www.webmd.com/balance/guide/choosing-to-be-happy

Whitley, Deborah M., PhD, Kelly, Susan J., PhD. "Grandparents Raising Grandchildren: A Call to Action," published on the Early Childhood Learning & Knowledge Center, p. 7, 9, 14 http://eclkc.ohs.acf.hhs.gov/hslc/tta-system/family/Family%20and%20Community%20Par

Wolfelt, Alan D., PhD. *Healing Your Grieving Heart for Teens: 100 Practical Ideas.* Fort Collins, CO: Companion Press, 2001. Entire book; no specific page numbers.

Wolfelt, Alan D., PhD. "Helping Teenagers cope With Grief," posted on the Grief Words website, http://griefwords.com/index.cgi?actoin=page&page=articles%2Fhelping25.html&site_id=202

Zero to Three website (National Center for Infants, Toddlers, and Families). "Temperament: Persistence, Patience, and Frustration," http://www.zerotothree.org/child-development/temperament-behavior/temperament-charact

Zucker, Bonnie, Dr. "Parents are Asking: Why is a Consistent Routine Important?," posted on the Parents Ask website, http://www.parentsask.com/articles/parents-are-asking-why-sonsistent-routine-important

Photo © 2011 by Haley Welby

ABOUT THE AUTHOR

Harriet Hodgson has been an independent journalist for more than 35 years. She is a member of the Association of Health Care Journalists, Association for Death Education and Counseling, and the Minnesota Coalition for Death Education and Support. She writes for two websites, a national magazine, is the author of hundreds of Internet/print articles, and 31 published books.

All of her writing comes from experience. A popular speaker, Hodgson has given presentations at Alzheimer's, hospice, and public health conferences. She also gives presentations to community groups about loss, recovery, and grandparenting. Hodgson has appeared on more than 160 radio talk shows, including CBS Radio, and dozens of television stations, including CNN.

Her work is cited in ***Who's Who of American Woman***, ***Who's Who in America***, ***World Who's Who of Women***, ***Contemporary Authors***, and other directories. Though her grandchildren are now in college, Hodgson continues to be involved in their lives and still considers herself a GRG. Hodgson lives in Rochester, Minnesota with her husband and twin grandchildren.

ALSO BY HARRIET HODGSON

- *Happy Again! Your New and Meaningful Life After Loss*

- *The Spiritual Woman: Quotes to Refresh and Sustain Your Soul*

- *101 Affirmations to Ease Your Grief Journey: Words of Comfort, Words of Hope*

- *Writing to Recover: The Journey from Loss and Grief to a New Life*

- *Writing to Recover Journal*

- *Smiling Through Your Tears: Anticipating Grief,* Lois Krahn, MD, co-author

Index

Behavior problems, 88
Berman, Diane, 88
Blair, Pamela, PhD, 22-23
Bolton, Robert, PhD, 55, 64, 66-67
Borba, Michele, EdD, 79

C
Caregving, age-appropriate, 39
Change, readiness for, 50-51
Cline, Foster W., MD, 24, 66, 87
Coffey, Laura, 44
College/university weekends, 85-86
Comments, responding to, 11-12
Communication, 53-55
Compliments, examples, 25, 56-57
Compliments, one-sentence, 25
Consistency, 57-58, 103
Creative outlets, 27-28

D
Dannison, Linda, PhD, 9, 58
Dartmouth Medical School, 117
Davies, Curt, 17
Daykin, Tom, 92
Denial, 29-30
Deits, Bob, 29, 85, 106, 134
Depression, 105-106
Divorce, 4-5
Dreams, disturbing, 25-26
Dyer, Kirsti A., MD, 105

Made in the USA
Middletown, DE
07 April 2016